THE UNI

DRAMA CLASSICS

The Dra[...] [...]ssics series aims to [...] [...] world's greatest
plays in a[...] [...]dents, actors
and thea[...] [...]s are accessible
introduct[...] [...]l theatrical
perspectiv[...]

Given tha[...] [...]ncountering a particular play
for the first time, the introduction seeks to fill in the
theatrical/historical background and to outline the chief
themes rather than concentrate on interpretational and
textual analysis. Similarly the play-texts themselves are free
of footnotes and other interpolations: instead there is an
end-glossary of 'difficult' words and phrases.

The texts of the English-language plays in the series
have been prepared taking full account of all existing
scholarship. The foreign-language plays have been newly
translated into a modern English that is both actable and
accurate: many of the translators regularly have their work
staged professionally.

Edited until his early death by Kenneth McLeish, the
Drama Classics series continues with his aim of providing a
first-class library of dramatic literature representing the best
of world theatre.

Associate editors:
Professor Trevor R. Griffiths
Visiting Professor in Humanities, Universities of Exeter and
Hertfo[...]
Dr C[...]
School[...]
Londo[...]

DRAMA CLASSICS *the first hundred*

*The publishers welcome
suggestions for further titles*

DRAMA CLASSICS

THE
UBU PLAYS

by
Alfred Jarry

translated and introduced by
Kenneth McLeish

NICK HERN BOOKS
London

www.nickhernbooks.co.uk

A Drama Classic

The Ubu Plays first published in Great Britain in this translation
as a paperback original in 1997 by Nick Hern Books Limited,
14 Larden Road, London W3 7ST. Reprinted 2000, 2006, 2010

Typeset by Country Setting, Kingsdown, Kent CT14 8ES
Printed by CPI Bookmarque, Croydon, Surrey

A CIP catalogue record for this book is available from the British Library

ISBN-13: 978 1 85459 189 0

Contents

Translator's Note

The translation of *Ubu Roi* printed here was commissioned by
Hilary Norrish for the BBC World Service, and was first
performed in her production by a cast including Alan Armstrong,
Alan Corduner, Pip Donaghy, Richard Pearce, Alison Peebles
and Emily Richard. The first stage production, at the Gate
Theatre, London in April 1997, was directed by John Wright,
designed by David Roger and performed by Allison Cologna,
Frazer Corbyn, Mark Stuart Currie, Stephen Finegold, Jonathan
Ferguson, Joanna Holden, Jonny Hoskins, Richard Katz and
Asta Sighvats.

Introduction

Alfred Henri Jarry (1873-1907)

Jarry was born and brought up in the provinces, but went to Paris at eighteen to study philosophy. (His professor was the famous Henri Bergson.) Already comic writing was his passion. From the age of twelve onwards he had composed verse, playlets, and nonsense-stories parodying the fiction of the time: typical titles are *The Umbrella-Syringe of Doctor Death, Roupias Tsunami-head* and *Fishing Overture.* At the same age, in company with two school friends, he had also amused himself by writing satirical sketches about his schoolteachers, and one of these, *The Poles,* was later reworked as *King Ubu (Ubu roi),* first play in the Ubu cycle.

The extraordinary energy of the three Ubu plays, and their cult status in European drama, have all but eclipsed everything else Jarry wrote or did. From student days onwards he supported himself as a writer, producing everything from reviews and satirical essays to music-hall songs, from mock philosophy to fiction. His 'novels' *The Supermale* and *The Exploits and Opinions of Doctor Faustroll, Pataphysician* are absurd masterpieces, anticipating the stories of Jorge Luis Borges or Italo Calvino on the one hand, and the satires of Stephen Leacock, James Thurber and Flann O'Brien on the other. The more people laughed, the more seriously he set his face, pretending that he was a genuine philosophical visionary and developing the spoof system of pataphysics. This, he said, was a 'science of imaginary solutions, which symbolically attributes the properties of objects, described by their virtuality, to their lineaments' – that is, one in which appearance is reality, and vice versa. (Its origins are the infants' game of 'No means Yes', and its implications are worked out before our eyes in *Slave Ubu.*)

In daily life, Jarry was eccentric in the gentle, melancholic vein also favoured by his contemporary, the composer Erik Satie. He was just under five feet tall and slight, dressed always in black and sported long black hair and a pointed beard which made him look like a miniature Mephistopheles. With a group of like-minded friends, he cultivated the art of living, as he put it, for the 'exquisite moment', of taking very seriously the business of taking nothing seriously at all. He rode a bicycle excitedly and energetically, as if it were a charger, sometimes into bars and houses as well as in the street. In admiration of Buffalo Bill, one of his heroes, he shot lighted cigarettes from people's mouths – with a popgun. He alternated between dandyism and never washing.

Jarry loved to play the part of Pa Ubu in real life, swaggering like a foul-mouthed little boy in a playground, indulging in orgies of food and, most especially, drink. He was an exponent of street theatre, happy to stand up and lecture passersby on insects, pataphysics, God, 'shikt' or any other subject that came into his head. He drank enormous quantities of absinthe, and took ether – experiments, he said, designed to lift his soul into a state of transcendental perception. When these practices destroyed his health and he fell mortally ill, he refused treatment on the grounds that he preferred illness to the mercies of 'merdecin'. On his sickbed, he had himself photographed as a corpse and sent his friends the photos as souvenirs.

What Happens in the Plays

In *King Ubu*, Pa Ubu is a cowardly toady, one of the hangers-on of Good King Wenceslas of Baloney. Nagged by his fearsome wife Ma Ubu, he gathers a band of Barmpots, led by the obnoxious Dogpile, assassinates Wenceslas and seizes the throne. He and the Barmpots fight Wenceslas's army, led by Princes Willy, Silly and Billikins, and defeat them. Billikins escapes to the hills, where the ghosts of his ancestors give him a great big sword and order him to organise resistance.

Ubu starts his reign by crawling to the people, but soon turns into a tyrant, debraining anyone who disagrees with him, murdering all the aristocrats and middle classes and extorting triple taxes from the peasants. The peasants revolt and go over to Billikins – and Dogpile, whom Ubu has rashly insulted, defects to Tsar Alexis of All the Russkies and leads him and his army to attack Baloney and restore Billikins to the throne. Ma Ubu steals the Balonian state treasure and a handsome Balonian soldier, and flees into exile.

Defeated in battle, Pa Ubu holes up in a cave with his cronies Wallop and McClub, and barely survives when a bear attacks them. Ma Ubu eventually reaches the same cave. She and Pa Ubu make up their differences, give up all claims to the Balonian throne and set off with Wallop and McClub on a voyage of exile to Engelland.

Cuckold Ubu (*Ubu cocu*) is the darkest and most surreal of the plays. Pa Ubu takes up residence in the home of Peardrop, a breeder of polyhedra, and he and his Barmpots tyrannise the neighbour-hood, despite the efforts of Pa Ubu's Conscience and Peardrop to stop them. There is war, led on Peardrop's side by Memnon (the singing Egyptian statue with whom Ma Ubu is cuckolding Pa Ubu) and by the banker Swankipants, and eventually a crocodile appears in true Punch-and-Judy style to chase off all the others. (We don't know whether it does or not: the play as it survives is incomplete.)

In *Slave Ubu* (*Ubu enchaîné*, 'Ubu in chains') Pa Ubu decides that he has had enough of tyranny, and that the only way to be free is to become a slave. He attaches himself and Ma Ubu to the dear old man Peebock and his daughter Eleutheria, and rules their household. The Three Free Men and their Sergeant Pisseasy (Eleutheria's fiancé) come to the rescue, and Ma and Pa Ubu are transferred to jail, preparatory to being sold as galley-slaves to Sultan Suleiman of Turkishland. The jail is so comfortable that the Three Free Men and the Populace break in to become convicts themselves. Two convoys of convicts set out to Turkishland, one consisting of the Ubs and the convicts (who have generously exchanged clothes and manacles with their guards) and the other led by Pisseasy. Sultan Suleiman makes them all galley slaves, and they row into the sunset and live happily ever after.

The Ubu Plays

It is common everywhere, but in France it has been a long-standing literary tradition, for bright adolescents to mock their schoolteachers. The eighteenth-century philosophers Voltaire and Rousseau were merciless about their tutors. Charles Bovary's classmates do it in Flaubert's novel *Madame Bovary* (perhaps in deference to Flaubert's own custom of inventing embarrassing and painful adventures, not for publication, for those of his characters he disliked). The tradition continues in 'grand' literature such as André Gide's novel *The Counterfeiters*, and in such not-so-grand literature as French children's comics. But Jarry's Ubu plays are the only case in which such lampoons survive to become adult obsessions, or are developed into such influential works of art.

The original skits were the work not of Jarry but of two of his friends, the brothers Charles and Henri Morin. Jarry soon joined in, giving the brothers' ideas literary edge and bite, and reworking them as playlets. The boys' favourite butt was a fat physics teacher, Monsieur Hébert, known to his pupils as 'Pa Ébé', 'Éb' and 'Ébouille'. Hébert, at least in his pupils' opinion, was a sadist, and Jarry later claimed that he was also the quintessence of bourgeois vulgarity, 'grotesquerie incarnate'. In the comedy sketch *The Poles*, written when the boys were fourteen and fifteen, Ébé has absurd, Rabelaisian adventures in Poland – and this material was reworked soon afterwards into the first version of *King Ubu*, in which Ubu's ambitious wife emulates Lady Macbeth and nags her husband into killing the King and usurping his throne.

This first version of *King Ubu* was first staged, by puppets, when Jarry was fifteen. It seems to have obsessed him from that moment onwards, and he spent much of the next three years adding material, polishing, illustrating, writing songs and making stage designs. As soon as he went to Paris, he sent the play (now substantially as it survives) to Aurélien-Marie Lugné-Poë, the *avant-garde* actor and director who had brought Ibsen's *Peer Gynt* to France and was involved with such experimental writers as the early symbolists, especially Maurice Maeterlinck. Lugné-Poë mounted a performance by live actors of *King Ubu* in 1896, and his and Jarry's production (involving masks, costumes of painted cardboard, hobby-horses, and the dehumanisation, or perhaps one should say puppetisation, of the actors), not to mention the play's very first word (*merdre*, 'shikt'), outraged the bourgeois audience and caused a scandal not matched until the première of Stravinsky's *Rite of Spring* nearly two decades later. In 1898 the play was revived in a puppet theatre belonging to Jarry's friend, the painter Pierre Bonnard, and yet another revision, *Up Ubu* (*Ubu sur la butte*), was performed by the marionettes of the Théâtre guignol des gueules de bois in 1901: see Appendix, page 124. The 'sequels' *Cuckold Ubu* and *Slave Ubu* were written in the 1890s and performed in various versions during that time. Jarry never produced a definitive version of *Cuckold Ubu*; *Slave Ubu* was first published in 1900.

The Ubu plays, and particularly *King Ubu*, quickly became one of the most influential *avant-garde* creations of the new century. Generations of writers, painters, musicians and above all theatre writers and performers were inspired by the way Jarry pushed parody and inconsequentiality to a point where the work seemed to exist only in its own self-created, lunatic world, with an arrogant sure-footedness that had nothing to do with anything which had existed earlier. Among the movements owing debts to the plays were Cubism, Dada, Expressionism, Futurism, Surrealism and the Theatre of the Absurd. Their influence can be traced right to such individual creations as the Marx Brothers films and *Hellzapoppin'* in the 1930s, the Goon Show and 'Mad' magazine in the 1950s, Monty Python's Flying Circus and films such as *Airplane* and the 'Naked Gun' series in the 1980s. Jarry's work liberated other people's creative imagination. His irreverence towards pre-existing culture, to his audience, his performers and the world at large, and the plays' absolute self-certainty – what Jarry called *je m'en foutisme* ('stuffyouism') – prefigured a whole twentieth-century approach to the arts and their audiences, first in Europe and then throughout the world.

The Ubu plays' dehumanisation of actors, their surrealism, parody and linguistic experimentation may nowadays seem to us to be absolutely characteristic of a particular time and style in the arts: the first of many challenges flung in the face of nineteenth-century creative certainties and the eager adoption of experiment of all kinds which marked the turn of the twentieth century. But the plays' power to shock outlasted the age of their creation and outranked all imitations. In the 1980s, when communist tyrannies began to collapse throughout Eastern Europe, *King Ubu* was a favourite theatre text everywhere, and was talked of not as a piece of pure fun but as a forceful and subversive political allegory. Throughout the plays' life they have had – and perhaps still have today – extraordinary power not only to entertain, but to make their audiences think. Without a single Brechtian inflection, they are supreme examples of what he called dialectical theatre – except that, characteristically of Jarry, they preach no message but allow you to read into them any ideas you like, or none at all.

The Puppet Tradition

Jarry was quite happy if people were outraged by his Ubu plays or dismissed them (as one contemporary critic did) as no more than 'iconoclastic exhibitionism'. He wrote tongue-in-cheek articles and gave lectures disclaiming the controversies while vigorously stoking them. But in fact, the plays' style has far simpler origins than the desire to shock. They are those of the European puppet theatre, with its centuries-old tradition of satirical outspokenness and grotesquerie. This existed from medieval times, when performances by live actors were first banned by the Christian authorities, and survived both in popular forms (such as Punch and Judy or Kharaghiozis) and in upper-class puppet entertainments drawing inspiration from the *commedia dell'arte* and *The Arabian Nights* – almost every European 'great house' in the sixteenth and seventeenth centuries had its puppet theatre.

Jarry was an expert on this tradition. He gave puppet performances from his early teens, and in 1893 wrote a prize-winning essay on the Guignol (marionette) tradition in Europe. He always preferred puppet performances of the Ubu plays to live ones, and when live productions *were* mounted, he used every technique of puppet staging to make his actors look like marionettes – except, as he innocently pointed out to one audience, attaching strings to their arms and legs, 'which would be ridiculous'. Guignol characters – the swashbuckling Knight, the Blackamoor, the Egyptian, the crocodile, the cutout army and especially the grotesque, stick-wielding anarchist at the heart of the action and his nagging, put-upon (and sometimes beaten-up) wife – are a main part of Jarry's inspiration, and the guignol style (later also used in silent film slapstick) of performing, deadpan, the wildest, most lunatic inventions, gives his plays their life.

Language

The language of the plays, similarly, has far less 'iconoclastic' origins than one might imagine. Jarry's characters speak for most of the time in playground slang, larded with secret words, puns and cocky, never-quite-gutter vocabulary (of which 'shikt', the plays' favourite rude word, is an example). Rabelais is a powerful influence – in later life, Jarry wrote a stage treatment of Rabelais' novel *Pantagruel*, and the imaginary France, Baloney, Russkiland and Engelland of the Ubu plays, with their posturing grandees, 'poofiprofs' and bourgeois fascination with huge meals and rivers of drink, are close to Rabelais' invented Abbey Thélème ('Do as you Please'), the goal to which all characters in *Pantagruel* progress. The chief difference is that although Pa Ubu shares with Rabelais' characters an obsession with money, blood, guts and the chamber pot, he is largely indifferent to that other great Rabelaisian appetite: for sex. At the same time, Jarry's scenes and dialogue keep veering into literary parody: of Shakespeare, Victor Hugo (author of *Les misérables* and *The Hunchback of Nôtre-Dame*), the melodramas of Sardou, academic treatises on science and philosophy, the swashbuckling novels of Alexandre Dumas (especially *The Three Musketeers*) and the pious Lives of the Holy Saints and Martyrs published by the Roman Catholic Church in Jarry's time. As the action progresses, language (especially Pa Ubu's) seems to collapse altogether, words coalescing and imploding as if dream were taking over from (what passes for) reality. Even the plays' ferocious gusto – they never stop, splattergunning the audience with cleverness – has what is really no more than schoolboy verve.

Location of the Action

The skits from which *King Ubu* was born were set in Pologne ('Poland'), and Jarry kept this location in the play, to give a kind of feudal, knightly resonance which he sent up in the battle and court scenes. But in a lecture given before the 1896 performance, he said that his 'Poland' was actually 'Nowhere at all', a surreal, invented place – and *pologne* is also French for a particularly phallic kind of sausage, rather like the salamis and 'German' sausages which feature in English pantomime and Punch and Judy shows. In this translation, I have renamed Poland Baloney and made other consequent changes. The other two plays are set in a France as imaginary as JohnBullLand might be to an English satirist. The English names in this translation are versions of similar puns or slangy distortions in the original French.

Kenneth McLeish, 1997

For Further Reading

Jarry is scandalously undervalued in English. The best book, Roger Shattuck's *The Banquet Years* (1959) deals with the epoch, not just the man, and is now four decades old. K.S. Beaumont, *Alfred Jarry: a Critical and Biographical Study* (1984) is rather po-faced for its subject, but covers all the ground. Martin Esslin, in *Theatre of the Absurd* (1962), is brief but good both on Jarry and his influence in later *avant-garde* theatre.

Jarry's novels *The Supermale* and *Exploits and Opinions of Doctor Faustroll, Pataphysician* were both published in English in the 1960s, and are 'useful' as well as fascinating and enjoyable. For those who read French, the Livre de Poche collection *Tout Ubu* is precisely what its title claims, and Henri Béhar's books *Jarry, le monstre et la marionette* (1973) and *Jarry dramaturge* (1980) are excellent critical studies.

Jarry: Key Dates

1873   Born.

1879-88 At school in Saint-Brieuc.

1885   Begins to write.

1888-91 At school in Rennes.

1888   First script of *The Poles*.

1891-3 Student in Paris.

1894-5 Military service (invalided out).

1895   Mercure de France publishes (first in sections, then complete) *Caesar-Antichrist*, a play made up of scenes from *King Ubu*.

1896   First production of *King Ubu*; scandal; first publication under its own name.

1898   Marionette production, at Pierre Bonnard's theatre. Jarry publishes a 'pseudo-pornographic' novelette, which includes part of *Cuckold Ubu*.

1900   *Slave Ubu* published.

1901   *Ubu sur la butte* first produced; novel *Messalina* published.

1902   *The Supermale*.

1903   Jarry working on *Pantagruel* and a comic opera about Pope Joan.

1906   Jarry falls mortally ill.

1907   Dies.

KING UBU

Characters

PA UBU
MA UBU
DOGPILE
GOOD KING WENCESLAS
QUEEN ROSAMOND
PRINCE WILLY
PRINCE SILLY
PRINCE BILLIKINS
BIG BAD BERNIE
WALLOP
McCLUB
FAST FREDDIE
NORBERT NURDLE
TSAR ALEXIS OF ALL THE RUSSKIES
NICK NACKERLEY
GENERAL CUSTARD
MAJOR F. FORT
BEAR

Barmpots, bankers, cashhounds, chaps, citizens, clerks,
councillors, flunkeys, ghosts, guards, judges, messengers,
nobs, partisans, seafarers, soldiers, turnkeys.

Act One

1 PA UBU, MA UBU.

PA UBU. Shikt.

MA UBU. Pa Ubu, language.

PA UBU. Watch it, Ma Ubu. I'll bash your head in.

MA UBU. Not my head, Pa Ubu. Someone else's.

PA UBU. Stagger me sideways, what d'you mean?

MA UBU. Come on, Pa Ubu. You *like* what you are?

PA UBU. Stagger me sideways, girl, of course I like it. Shikt, who wouldn't? Captain of the Guard, Eye and Ear of Good King Wenceslas, Past President of the Battalions of Baloney, Thane of Four-door. What more d'you want?

MA UBU. You're joking. Thane of Four-door, you used to be. Now who follows you? Fifty sausage-knotters in procession. Forget Four-door. Get your loaf measured for the crown of Baloney.

PA UBU. Ma Ubu, what are you on about?

MA UBU. As if you didn't know.

PA UBU. Stagger me sideways. Good King Wenceslas is still alive, for starters. And even if he wasn't, he's got a million kids.

MA UBU. So, do in the lot of them. Take over.

PA UBU. Watch it, Ma Ubu, or it's jug for you.

MA UBU. Idiot! If I'm in jug, who'll patch your pants?

PA UBU. So let 'em *see* my bum.

MA UBU. No: plant it on a throne. Just think of it. A pile of cash, big as you like. Bangers for breakfast. A golden coach.

PA UBU. If I was king, I'd have a big hat. Like that one I had in Four-door, till those bastards nicked it.

MA UBU. *And* a brolly. *And* a cloak so long that it brushed the floor.

PA UBU. I can't resist. Shickastick, if I catch him on his own, he's for it.

MA UBU. At last, Pa Ubu. A proper man at last.

PA UBU. Just a minute. I'm Captain of the Guard. Murder Good King Wenceslas? His Maj of Baloney? I'd rather die.

MA UBU (*aside*). Shikt. (*aloud*) You want to be Daddy Mouse forever? *Poor* Daddy Mouse?

PA UBU. Blubberit, stagger me sideways, I'd rather be poor, honest Daddy Mouse than Big Fat Cat that Nicked the Cream.

MA UBU. What about the brolly? The cloak? The great big hat?

PA UBU. What about them, Ma Ubu?

He goes, slamming the door.

MA UBU. Snikt, what a tight-arse. Never mind. Slipalipt, I'm loosening him. With God's good help, not to mention mine, I'll be Queen of Baloney by Saturday.

2   *Room in* PA UBU's *house, with a table set for a feast.* PA UBU, MA UBU.

MA UBU. Well, they're late. Our guests.

PA UBU. Yes. Stagger me sideways, I'm starving. Ma Ubu, you look really ugly today. Because we've got company?

MA UBU (*shrugging*). Shikt.

PA UBU (*grabbing a roast chicken*). Dagit, I'm hungry. I'll get stuck into this. Chicken, right? Snot bad.

MA UBU. Put that down. Leave something for the guests.

PA UBU. There's plenty. I won't touch another thing. Look out the window, Ma Ubu. See if our guests are here.

MA UBU (*going to the window*). No sign of them.

PA UBU snatches his chance and snitches a slice of meat.

Here they are. Captain Dogpile and his Barmpots. Pa Ubu, what are you eating?

PA UBU. Nothing. Collops.

MA UBU. Collops. Collops. Dagnagit, put them down!

PA UBU. Stagger me sideways, I'll dot you one.

The door opens.

3 PA UBU, MA UBU, DOGPILE, BARMPOTS.

MA UBU. Good evening, gents. So naice to see you. Do sit down.

DOGPILE. Ma Ubu, good evening. Where's Pa Ubu?

PA UBU. Here! Godnagit, stagger me sideways, I'm not that small.

DOGPILE. Good evening, Pa Ubu. Lads, siddown.

All sit.

PA UBU. Pff! Any bigger, I'd have smashed the chair.

DOGPILE. Oi, Ma Ubu, what's for dinner?

MA UBU. I'll tell you.

PA UBU. I like this part.

MA UBU. Baloney soup. Calfcollops. Chicken. Pâté de dog. Turkey bum. Charlotte Russe.

PA UBU. That's enough. Snurk! More?

MA UBU (*continuing*). Ice cream, lettuce, apples, hotpot, tartyfarts, cauliflower shikt.

PA UBU. Dagnagit, I'm paying for this. What d'you take me for, a bank?

MA UBU. Ignore him. He's barmy.

PA UBU. I'll barm your bum.

MA UBU. Shut up, Pa Ubu. Eat your burger.

PA UBU. Burger me, it's bad.

DOGPILE. Bleah, it's horrible.

MA UBU. Nagnancies, what d'you *want*?

PA UBU (*striking his forehead*). Got it! Hang on. I won't be long.

Exit.

MA UBU. Nah, gents, collops.

DOGPILE. Very nice. All gone.

MA UBU. Some turkeybum?

DOGPILE. Fantastic. Great! Up Ma Ubu.

ALL. Up Ma Ubu.

PA UBU *returns, carrying a disgusting brush.*

PA UBU. What about three cheers for Pa Ubu?

He pokes the brush at the guests.

MA UBU. Idiot, what are you doing?

PA UBU. It's lovely. Taste it, taste it.

Several of them taste and die, poisoned.

PA UBU. Ma Ubu, pass the tartyfarts. I'll hand them round.

MA UBU. Here.

PA UBU. Out, out, the lot of you. Captain Dogpile, I want a word.

THE OTHERS. Hey! We haven't finished.

PA UBU. Oh yes you have. Out, out! Dogpile, sit.

No one moves.

Still here? Stagger me sideways, where are those tartyfarts? I'll see to you.

He starts hurling tartyfarts.

ALL. Erg! Foo! Aagh!

PA UBU. Shikt, shikt, shikt. D'you get it? Out!

ALL. Bastard! Swine!

PA UBU. They've gone. What a lousy dinner. Dogpile, walkies.

Exeunt.

4   PA UBU, MA UBU, DOGPILE.

PA UBU. Here, Dogpile. Diddums like oo dindins?

DOGPILE. Lovely. All but the shikt.

PA UBU. The shikt was great.

MA UBU. Shickun son goo. That's French.

PA UBU. Captain Dogpile, I'm going to make you Lord de Lawdy.

DOGPILE. Pardon, Pa Ubu? I thought you were skint.

PA UBU. In a day or two, with your help, I'll be King of Baloney.

DOGPILE. You're going to kill Good King Wenceslas?

PA UBU. Aren't you the clever one?

DOGPILE. If you're doing for Good King Wenceslas, count me in. I'm his mortal enemy. Me and my Barmpots.

PA UBU (*falling on his neck*). Dogpile! Darling!

DOGPILE. Puah, you stink, Pa Ubu. Don't you ever wash?

PA UBU. What if I don't?

MA UBU. He doesn't know how to.

PA UBU. I'll stample you.

MA UBU. Shiktface.

PA UBU. Out, Dogpile. That's all for now. I'll make you Lord de Lawdy. That's a promise. Stagger me sideways, I swear, on Ma Ubu's head.

MA UBU. Hey . . .

PA UBU. Shut it, girl.

Exeunt.

5   PA UBU, MA UBU, MESSENGER.

PA UBU. Hey you. What is it? Piss off. Who needs you?

MESSENGER. Sirrah, you're summoned. By his Majesty.

Exit.

PA UBU. Oh shikt. Dogalmighty, stagger me sideways, they know. I'm done for. Chopped. Oh dear.

MA UBU. You great jelly. Get on with it.

PA UBU. I know, I'll say it was her . . . and that Dogpile.

MA UBU. Lardbelly, just you try.

PA UBU. Just watch me.

He goes. MA UBU *runs after him.*

MA UBU. Pa Ubu! No! Pa Ubu! I'll let you have sausage.

PA UBU (*off*). Sausage, ha! Haha! HaHA!

6 *The royal palace.* GOOD KING WENCESLAS, *surrounded by his officers*; DOGPILE; *princes* SILLY, WILLY *and* BILLIKINS. *Enter* PA UBU.

PA UBU. It was them, not me. Ma Ubu, Dogpile. They did it.

KING. Did what, Pa Ubu?

DOGPILE. He's pissed.

KING. One knows how it feels.

PA UBU. Of course I'm pissed. From drinking toasts.

KING. Pa Ubu, it is our purpose to reward your loyal service as Captain of the Guard. From this day on, be known as Baron Stretcholand.

PA UBU. Good ole Majesty, how kind, how kind.

KING. Never mind all that, Pa Ubu. Just turn up at the Posh Parade tomorrow.

PA UBU. I will, I will. But first, your Maj . . . a little gift.

He gives him a kazoo.

KING. A kazoo? What shall we do with it? We'll give it to Billikins.

BILLIKINS. Pa Ubu's orf his chump.

PA UBU. Right, 'scuse me, time to piss off.

He turns and falls.

Gor! Nyai! Stagger me sideways, I've knackered my kneecap and gurdled my gob.

KING (*getting up*). I say, Pa Ubu, are you all right?

PA UBU. All right? I'm done for. What'll become of poor old Ma?

KING. One shall look after her.

PA UBU. How kind. But don't think that'll save you.

Exit.

7   PA UBU'*s house*. PA UBU, MA UBU, BIG BAD BERNIE, WALLOP, McCLUB, DOGPILE, BARMPOTS, SOLDIERS.

PA UBU. OK, lads. Time to get this plot moving. Who's got an idea? Me first. Me first.

DOGPILE. Pa Ubu, go on.

PA UBU. This is it, lads. It's simple. I stuff his lunch with arsenic. He shoves it down his gob, drops dead, and I nab his throne.

ALL. Ooh! Cheeky monkey! Aren't you the naughty one?

PA UBU. Good, innit? Dogpile, got anything better?

DOGPILE. I suggest: one slash of the sabre, to slice him in snippets from snitch to shoe.

ALL. Yay! Our hero! Whee! Yeehah!

PA UBU. And suppose he kicks you up the bum? Have you forgotten those stout iron shoes he wears for Posh Parades? In any case, now I know, I'll tell him. There'll be a big reward.

MA UBU. Coward, traitor, lardbag.

ALL. Boo! Hiss!

PA UBU. Watch it, or I'll drop you lot in as well. Oh, all right. For your sakes, lads, I'll do it. Dogpile, stand by to slice.

DOGPILE. Hang on. Why don't we all pile in on him, yelling and shouting? We've got to scare off his guards.

PA UBU. Got it! I stamp on his toe. He kicks me. I shout 'SHIKT' – and that's the signal. You all pile in.

MA UBU. Then as soon as he's dead, you grab the crown.

DOGPILE. And I and the lads see to the rest of them.

PA UBU. Right. Especially that bastard Billikins.

They start to go. He drags them back.

Hang on. Haven't we forgotten something? The solemn oath?

DOGPILE. How do we do that, without a bible?

PA UBU. We'll use Ma Ubu. Swear on her.

ALL. Yay. Good. Right.

PA UBU. OK. You all swear to kill Good King Wenceslas . . . properly?

ALL. We swear. We'll kill him. Up Pa Ubu. Yay.

End of Act One.

Act Two

1 *The royal palace.* GOOD KING WENCESLAS, QUEEN ROSAMOND, SILLY, WILLY, BILLIKINS.

KING. Prince Billikins, this morning you were very cheeky to Pa Ubu, one's Captain of the Guard, one's Baron Stretcholand. One therefore grounds you. Stay away from one's Posh Parade.

QUEEN. Hang on, Wence. You need the whole family there. Security.

KING. One means what one says. Don't bibblebabble, madam. You tire one's ears.

BILLIKINS. Mighty majesty, pater: one submits.

QUEEN. You're really going through with it, your Maj? This Posh Parade?

KING. Madam, why not?

QUEEN. I told you before. I had a dream. He smote you with his smiters, chucked you in the river and nabbed the crown. That lion and unicorn put it on his head.

KING. Whose head?

QUEEN. Pa Ubu's head.

KING. Absurd. His Lord High Ubuness is the soul of loyalty. He'd let wild horses mangle him to mincemeat before he harmed a hair of one's head.

QUEEN, BILLIKINS. You're just so *wrong*.

KING. Enough. We'll show you how much one trusts Count Ubu. One will attend the Posh Parade dressed just as one is. No sword, no armour.

QUEEN. Alack! O woe! I'll not clap eyes on you no moe.

KING. Come, Willy. Come Silly.

They go. The QUEEN *and* BILLIKINS *go to the window.*

QUEEN, BILLIKINS. God and St Nick protect you.

QUEEN. Billikins, come with me to church. We'll pray for them.

2   *The parade ground. The* BALONIAN ARMY, GOOD KING
WENCESLAS, WILLY, SILLY, PA UBU, DOGPILE *and his*
BARMPOTS, BIG BAD BERNIE, WALLOP, McCLUB.

KING. Baron Ubu, stand beside one, you and your chaps. It's
time to inspect the troops.

PA UBU (*aside to his men*). Any minute now. (*to the* KING) Right
behind you, sire.

UBU'*s men gather round the* KING.

KING. Ah! The Forty-seventh Mounted Foot and Mouth. Aren't
they something?

PA UBU. They're rubbish. Look at that one, there. Oi, monkey's
armpit, have you forgotten how to shave?

KING. He looks smooth enough to one. Pa Ubu, what's up?

PA UBU. This.

He stamps on his foot.

KING. Bastard.

PA UBU. SHIKT! It's time!

DOGPILE. Pile on, lads.

They all attack the KING. *One* BARMPOT *explodes.*

KING. One's done for! Help! One's dead.

WILLY (*to* SILLY). I say. Up and at 'em, what?

PA UBU. I've got the crown. See to the rest of them.

DOGPILE. Get the bastards. Now!

The PRINCES *run for it. All chase them.*

3   QUEEN ROSAMOND, BILLIKINS.

QUEEN. Oh that's better. I love a good pray.

BILLIKINS. There's nothing to be afraid of.

Huge shouting, off.

What's that? I say, my brothers. Pa Ubu and his badlads, after them.

QUEEN. God save us. Saints and martyrs! They're gaining on them.

BILLIKINS. The whole bally army, following Pa Ubu. Where's his Majesty? Oh! I say!

QUEEN. Willy's down. Poor Willy's shot.

BILLIKINS. Silly!

SILLY *turns.*

Look out!

QUEEN. He's surrounded.

BILLIKINS. He's done for. Dogpile's sliced him like salami.

QUEEN. Saints and martyrs! They've broken into the palace. They're climbing the stairs. They're foaming at the mouth.

QUEEN, BILLIKINS (*on their knees*). God save us. Please.

BILLIKINS. If I get my hands on that bounder Ubu . . .

4   *The same. The door is broken down.* PA UBU *and the*
BARMPOTS *burst in.*

PA UBU. Yeah, Billikins? What will you do?

BILLIKINS. Good god, man, I'll defend my mater. To the last
drop of blood. Take one step further, make one's day.

PA UBU. Dogpile, I'm scared. I'm off.

SOLDIER (*advancing*). Billikins, on guard!

BILLIKINS. On guard yourself.

He bops his bonce.

QUEEN. Bully for Billy! One for you!

OTHERS (*advancing*). We'll see to you, Billikins. We'll take good
care of you.

BILLIKINS. Bounders! Ruffians! Take that! And that!

He whirls his sabre and massacres them.

PA UBU. He's a slinky little slicer. But that won't save his bacon.

BILLIKINS. Mater, escape by the secret passage.

QUEEN. What about you, son? What about you?

BILLIKINS. I'll follow.

PA UBU. Grab the queen. Oh, she's gone. Right, you bastard . . .

He advances on BILLIKINS.

BILLIKINS. Cry God for Billikins and Sangorge!

He nicks UBU's *napper with a savage swordslice.*

Mater, wait for me!

He escapes by the secret passage.

5 *A cave in the mountains.* BILLIKINS, QUEEN ROSAMOND.

BILLIKINS. We'll be quite safe here.

QUEEN. Oh, Billikins. Ah.

She falls on the snow.

BILLIKINS. What's the matter, mater?

QUEEN. I'm ill, Bill. I've only two hours to live.

BILLIKINS. Good lord. Hypothermia?

QUEEN. So many blows. How could I endure? His majesty
murdered, our family finished – and you, last remnant of the
royal race, forced to flee, here in the hills, like a common
catnapper.

BILLIKINS. And forced by *him*, what's more. That bounder
Ubu. That oik. That swine. When I think how the pater
larded him with honours, lorded him – for this! The very next
morning, a knife in the guts. That's hardly cricket. Not fair at
all.

QUEEN. Oh Billikins, remember how happy we were before Pa
Ubu came! Ah me, what a change is here.

BILLIKINS. Chin up, mater. We'll bide our time. We'll watch
for the sunrise. We'll remember who we are.

QUEEN. The sunrise! Ah child, for you perhaps, glad dawn. But
these poor eyes won't live to see it.

BILLIKINS. What's up? She's white. She's limp. Anyone there?
I say . . . ? Oh lord, her heart's not beating. She's dead.
Good grief, yet another of Pa Ubu's victims.

He hides his face in his hands and sobs.

It isn't fair. Alone at fourteen years old, with such violent
vengeance to bally bear.

*He surrenders himself to the most violent despair. Meanwhile, the ghosts
of* GOOD KING WENCESLAS, SILLY, WILLY *and*
QUEEN ROSAMOND, *plus their* ANCESTORS, *fill the cave.*

The senior GHOST *goes to* BILLIKINS *and prods him tenderly.*

GHOST. Bear with me, Billikins. In life, I was Vaslav the
    Versatile, first king and founder of our royal line. To you,
    now, I hand this holy task: our vengeance.

He gives him a big sword.

And this great big sword. Let it not rest nor sleep till that
    traitor dieth, till it encompasseth his death.

All the GHOSTS *disappear, leaving* BILLIKINS *in a state of
    exaltation.*

6 *The royal palace.* PA UBU, MA UBU, DOGPILE.

PA UBU. I bloody will not. Bumbrains! Why should I bankrupt
    myself for them?

DOGPILE. It's traditional, Pa Ubu. Coronation . . . goodies for
    everyone. People expect it.

MA UBU. Loads to eat, a mint of money, or you'll be out by
    Tuesday.

PA UBU. Mintomoney, no. Loadsteat, fine. Knacker three old
    nags. That's good enough for lardipuffs like them.

MA UBU. Look who's talking. Lardipuffs!

PA UBU. I keep telling you, I'm here to make my pile. Mine,
    every penny, mine.

MA UBU. You've got the Balonian Big Bank. What more d'you
    want?

DOGPILE. I know. In the cathedral. There's hidden treasure. I
    know where it is. We'll give them that.

PA UBU. Just you try. One finger . . .

DOGPILE. Pa Ubu, unless you give them something, they'll never pay their taxes.

PA UBU. You're kidding.

MA UBU. No he's not.

PA UBU. Oh, all right. Do what you like. Three million cash, a billion chopsansteaks. Just leave some for me!

Exeunt.

7 *Palace courtyard, full of people.* PA UBU, *crowned.* MA UBU, DOGPILE, FLUNKEYS *staggering with meat.*

PEOPLE. Up Ubu. Hurray! Up Ubu. Yay!

PA UBU (*throwing gold*). There. There. I'm not doing this because I like it. It was Ma's idea. Be sure and pay your taxes.

ALL. We will. We will.

DOGPILE. Ma Ubu, look. They're fighting for the cash. It's hell down there.

MA UBU. Fooagh, look: he's had his brains bashed in.

PA UBU. Lovely! Bring more gold.

DOGPILE. Suppose we had a race?

PA UBU. Brilliant. (*to the* PEOPLE) Friends, you see this golden treasure chest? Stuffed with money. Thirty zillion nicker. Balonian bazoomas, every pee of it: no rubbish. Anyone who wants to be in the race, go over there. Start when I wave my hanky. First here gets the lot. If you don't win, the consolation prize is this other chest. You share it: everyone gets something.

ALL. Yeehah! God save the king. Up Ubu. It was never like this when Good King Wenceslas was king.

PA UBU (*joyfully to* MA UBU). Listen to them!

    The PEOPLE *line up at one side of the courtyard.*

    One, two, three. Are you ready?

ALL. Yes! Yes!

PA UBU. Go!

    They surge forward. Jostling, tumult.

DOGPILE. They're coming! They're coming!

PA UBU. Him in front, he's flagging.

MA UBU. No, he's not. Come on!

DOGPILE. Ah, he came too soon. Come on, the other one! Come on!

    The runner who had been second wins.

ALL. Fast Freddie! Hurray! Hurray!

FAST FREDDIE. Sire, what can I say? Your majesty, your majesty . . .

PA UBU. Tsk, it's nothing. Freddie, lovey, take your money. Enjoy. Mwah, mwah. And the rest of you, here's yours. One coin each, until they're done.

ALL. Yay! Fast Freddie, Pa Ubu! Hurray! Hurray!

PA UBU. All right, it's dinner time. You're all invited. In you go!

PEOPLE. In! Up Ubu! Hurray!

    They go into the palace. We hear the noise of revelry, and it lasts all night. Curtain.

    End of Act Two.

Act Three

1   *The palace.* PA UBU, MA UBU.

PA UBU. Stagger me sideways, I've dunnit: king. I've had the party . . . got the angover . . . Next, the great big cloak.

MA UBU. Very naice, Pa Ubu. It's naice being royal.

PA UBU. You said it, girl.

MA UBU. We've such a lot to thank him for.

PA UBU. Who?

MA UBU. Captain Dogpile. Lord de Lawdy.

PA UBU. Lord de Lawdy? You're joking. Now I don't need him any more, he can stuff his lordship.

MA UBU. Bad idea, Pa Ubu. He may turn nasty.

PA UBU. I'm so frightened! Him and that Billikins.

MA UBU. You've not frightened of Billikins?

PA UBU. Tickle me taxes, he's fourteen years old! A spottibot!

MA UBU. Pa Ubu, be careful. Be naice to him. Bribe him.

PA UBU. More money down the tubes! I've spent sixty squillion already.

MA UBU. I'm telling you, Billikins'll win. He's got justice fighting on his side.

PA UBU. So bloody what? We've got injustice, haven't we? You piss me off, Ma Ubu. I'll settle you.

He chases her out.

2   *Great hall of the palace.* PA UBU, MA UBU, OFFICERS,
SOLDIERS, BIG BAD BERNIE, WALLOP, McCLUB, NOBS
IN CHAINS, BANKERS, LAWYERS, CLERKS.

PA UBU. Bring the nob-box, the nob-hook, the nob-knife, the
   nob-ledger − and the nobs.

   The NOBS *are pushed forward, roughly.*

MA UBU. Pa Ubu, please. Go easy.

PA UBU. Listen up. Royal decree. To enrich the state, I'm going
   to do in all the nobs and snitch their loot.

NOBS. Ooh! Aah! Help!

PA UBU. Bring me Nob Number One. And the nob-hook. All
   those condemned to death, I shove down this hole. Down to
   the Slushpile to be debrained. (*to the* NOB) What's your name,
   dogbum?

NOB. Viscount of Vitebsk.

PA UBU. How much is that worth?

NOB. Three million a year.

PA UBU. Guilty!

   He hooks him down the chute.

MA UBU. You're so strict.

PA UBU. Next nob. What's your name?

   Silence.

   Answer, bogbrain.

SECOND NOB. Protector of Pinsk. Not to mention Minsk.

PA UBU. Ducky. Down you go. Next! What an ugly bastard.
   Who are you?

THIRD NOB. Holder of Hanover, Halle and Harrogate.

PA UBU. Three in one? Down the tube. Next nob. Name?

FOURTH NOB. Proud Palatine of Polock.

PA UBU. Pollocks to that, mate. Down the tube. What's biting you, Ma Ubu?

MA UBU. You're being so fierce.

PA UBU. I'm working. Making my fortune. I'll hear the list now. Clerk of the Court, MY list. MY titles. Read MY list to ME.

CLERK. Viscount of Vitebsk. Protector of Pinsk. Holder of Hanover, Halle, Harrogate. Palatine of Polock.

PA UBU. Yes. *Well . . . ?*

CLERK. That's all.

PA UBU. What d'you mean, that's all? Come here, nobs. The lot of you. I'm not rich enough yet, so you're all for the chop. You've got it, I need it. Stuff the nobs down the tube.

The NOBS *are stuffed down the hatch.*

Get a nurdle on. I've laws to pass.

SEVERAL. Big deal.

PA UBU. Lawyers first, then bankers.

SEVERAL LAWYERS. Objection! Nolle prosequi. Status quo.

PA UBU. Shikt. Law Number One: judges' salaries. Abolished.

JUDGES. What'll we live on? We're skint. All skint.

PA UBU. Live on the fines.

FIRST JUDGE. Impossible.

SECOND JUDGE. Outrageous.

THIRD JUDGE. Unheard-of.

FOURTH JUDGE. Beyond the pale.

JUDGES. Under these conditions, we refuse to judge.

PA UBU. All judges down the tube!

They struggle, in vain.

MA UBU. What're you doing, Pa Ubu? Who'll do the judging, now?

PA UBU. Watch and see. Who's next, now? Bankers.

BANKERS. No change!

PA UBU. First off, I want half of all charges.

BANKERS. You're joking.

PA UBU. And here *are* some charges: property, ten percent, commerce and industry, twenty-five percent, marriage and death fifty nicker each.

FIRST BANKER. Pa Ubu, it just isn't viable.

SECOND BANKER. It doesn't add up.

THIRD BANKER. Neither ult nor inst.

PA UBU. Take the piss, would you? Down the tube!

The BANKERS *are downchuted.*

MA UBU. Fine king you are, killing the whole world.

PA UBU. Don't worry, girl. I'll go from town to town myself, collect the cash.

3   *Rude hut in the Balonian countryside.* PEASANTS.

PEASANT (*entering*). I come with news. His majesty's no more. His sons no more. Save Billikins. He got away. His mummy too. They're in the hills. Pa Ubu's nabbed the throne.

ANOTHER PEASANT. And that's not all. I've just been to town and they were carting corpses and the corpses belonged to three hundred executed nobles and five hundred executed judges and they're doubling the taxes and Pa Ubu's coming to collect them in person.

ALL. Alack! What now? Pa Ubu's a rotten swine and his family's no better. Or so they say.

PEASANT. Hark! What's that? There's someone at the door.

PA UBU (*outside*). Rumblestuffsticks! Open up! By shikt, by Dikt, by good saint Nickt, cashknackers, slashpacks, I want your tax!

The door is broken down. UBU *bursts in, with a pack of* CASHHOUNDS.

4

PA UBU. Who's the oldest?

A PEASANT *steps forward.*

PEASANT. Norbert Nurdle.

PA UBU. Right. Listen. Rumblestuffsticks, I said listen. D'you want these frensomine to clip your clackers?

PEASANT. But your Majesty hasn't said anything.

PA UBU. Wrong, pal. I've been flapping my gob for the whole last hour. Fetch out your tax-pot, now, or die. Cashandlers, the cashcart.

The cashcart is brought in.

PEASANT. The point is, sire, we're covered by limited liability. The documents were based on an assessment of wundruntunty poundipees. And we paid in full, the Feast of St Multiple Ult.

PA UBU. So what? I've changed the rules. It was in the paper: all taxes to be paid twice over, except those I may dream up later, to be paid three times. Simple, innit? I make my fortune, snickersnack, then kill the whole world and buggeroff.

PEASANTS. Lord Ubu, have pity. We're honest, simple folk. We're poor.

PA UBU. Tough titty. Pay. Unless you want the rest of it. Neck-knotting, noodle-nackering. Rumblestuffsticks, I am the bloody king.

PEASANTS. You aren't. Revolution! Up Billikins. His majesty. The king.

PA UBU. Cashcarters, kill.

A battle begins. The house is wrecked. None escape except old NORBERT, who legs it across the plain. UBU is left alone, scooping cash.

5 *Dungeon.* UBU, *with* DOGPILE *in chains.*

PA UBU. It's just what happens, mate. You ask for what I owe you, I say no, you turn nasty, you end up here. Goldalmighty! It's perfect. Couldn't be better. You've got to agree.

DOGPILE. Pa Ubu, beware. Five days you've held this throne. You've killed. You just don't care. Dead corpses scream and groan for vengeance. Pa Ubu, beware.

PA UBU. Very good: a poet, and don't you know it. If you once got out of here . . . ! Oh yes, oh yes. How lucky for me that this dank deep dungeon, enclosed by craggy castle, has never popped a prisoner yet. Night night, sleep tight, keep hold of your nicker-nack, the rats here bite.

Exit. TURNKEYS *bolt all the doors.*

6 *Palace of* TSAR ALEXIS OF ALL THE RUSSKIES. TSAR ALEXIS, *his* COURTIERS, DOGPILE.

ALEXIS. Base mercenary wretch! Wast even thou who conspired to do in our good king cousin, Wenceslas?

DOGPILE. I'm sorry, sire. Pa Ubu made me. I didn't want to.

ALEXIS. Big liar. Never mind. What d'you want now?

DOGPILE. Pa Ubu dungeoned me for treason. I managed to escape. I've been on the road five days, five nights. Galloping. On a horse. To beg your royal pardon.

ALEXIS. What practical proof presentest thou?

DOGPILE. My soldier's sword. And this detailed plan of the castle.

ALEXIS. We accept the sword. But burn the plan, by Genghis. We'll not come top by cheating.

DOGPILE. One of good king Wenceslas' sons, young Billikins, still lives. To see him on the throne, I'd give my all.

ALEXIS. In the Brave Balonian Battalions, what place hadst thou?

DOGPILE. Commander of the fifth phalanx of fusiliers. Pa Ubu's personal protectors.

ALEXIS. OK. Thou'rt now lieutenant of lancers. Sub. If thou dost well, thou gets rewarded. If thou betray'st us, watch out.

DOGPILE. I lack not courage, sire.

ALEXIS. Good. Vanish from our presence. Scat.

Exit.

7   UBU's *council chamber.* PA UBU, MA UBU, COUNCILLORS.

PA UBU. Order. I declare this meeting open. Stretch your ears and flab your gobs. Agenda: one, cashcount. Two, my new idea: how to keep it sunny and do away with rain.

COUNCILLOR. Lord Ubu, brilliant.

MA UBU. Licker.

PA UBU. Queen of my shikt, button it. We're not doing badly, lords. Our brass-knuckle boys bring in the bacon. Our mother-muggers work miracles. Everywhere you look, you see nothing but houses crumbling and citizens grumbling under the burden of our bills.

COUNCILLOR. The new taxes, Lord Ubu. What about them?

MA UBU. They're rubbish. Tax on marriages: three pee. Pa Ubu's chasing people in the street and forcing them into church.

PA UBU. Stuffsticks! Chancelloress of the Exchequeress, I'm talking.

Enter MESSENGER

What's he want? Blugger off, cat-basket, or I'll trundle your trollops and snaggle your snipes.

MA UBU. Too late. He's gone. He left this postcard.

PA UBU. You read it. I'm depressed. I've forgotten how to read. Get a grundle on. It'll be from Dogpile.

MA UBU. So it is. 'Having a lovely taime. Tsar Alexis of all the Russkies really naice. Invading tomorrow to put Billikins back on throne and stuff your guts. Regards . . . '

PA UBU. I'm done for. The naughty man's coming to hurt me. St Nickerless, oelpme, I'll give you all my taxes. God, tell me what to do. I'll even pray. Oh what am I to do?

He sobs and sobs.

MA UBU. Pa Ubu, there's only one thing for it. War.

ALL. Hurrah! Fight! Yay!

PA UBU. Oh brilliant. Thrashed again.

FIRST COUNCILLOR. Call up the army.

SECOND COUNCILLOR. Lines of supply.

THIRD COUNCILLOR. Forts, cannons, balls.

FOURTH COUNCILLOR. Cash for our boys.

PA UBU. Ah! No. What d'you take me for? Me, pay? No chance. Stagger me sideways, we'll fight if you're all so eager. But pay? Not me.

ALL. War! War! Yay!

8 *In camp outside* UBU'*s capital city.* PA UBU, MA UBU, SOLDIERS, BARMPOTS.

SOLDIERS *and* BARMPOTS. Up Baloney! Up Ubu!

PA UBU. Ma Ubu, give me my breastplate. My poky-stick. I'll be so loaded, I won't be able to run if they're after me.

MA UBU. Coward.

PA UBU. Godnag this shikastick. This nobhook. They won't stay put. I'll never be ready. The Russkies'll come and kill me.

SOLDIER. Lord Ubu, your snackersnicks are falling down.

PA UBU. I dead you, hookynobbyshikastick. Slicymug. Piff, paff, pah.

MA UBU. What does he look like? His breastplate, his iron hat. Like an armour-plated pumpkin.

PA UBU. Time to mount. Bring forth Cashnag.

MA UBU. Whadyoo say?

PA UBU. Cashnag. My . . . charger.

MA UBU. He can't carry you. He's not been fed since Tuesday. He's a bag of bones.

PA UBU. You're joking. Twelve pee a day and still can't carry me? You're pulling my leg, cornswobbit, you're pocketing the cash.

MA UBU *blushes and lowers her eyes.*

Bring Cashnag Two. Rumblestuffsticks, I refuse to walk.

An enormous horse is brought in.

I'll mount. There's no air up here. I'm dizzy. I'll fall.

The horse moves off.

Help! Make it stand still. I'll fall.

MA UBU. What an idiot. He's on. He's off again.

PA UBU. Godnagit, I thought I'd had it that time. Never mind. I'm off. To war. I'll kill the whole world. Especially those who don't march in step. Ubu be angry, Ubu pullout oo teef, oo tongue.

MA UBU. Pa Ubu, farewell.

PA UBU. I forgot to tell you. Take over while I'm gone. I've got the cashledger with me, so keep your sticky hands to yourself, all right? I'm leaving Big Bad Bernie to look after you. Ma Ubu, farewell.

MA UBU. Pa Ubu, tata. Give that Tsar whatfor.

PA UBU. Watch me. Nose-knotting, teeth-twisting, tongue-tearing, noodlenackering.

Fanfares as the army marches off.

MA UBU (*alone*). Hangdock he's gone. Lardifard! Right. Get organised, kill Billikins and grab the loot.

End of Act Three.

Act Four

1 *Royal crypt in the cathedral.*

MA UBU. Where is it, the treasure? None of these stones sound
   hollow. I've done it right: thirteen steps along the wall from
   the tomb of Vaslav the Versatile. Just a minute: this one
   sounds hollow. Ma Ubu, to work! Prise it open. Mff! Won't
   budge. I'll use the cashook. It's never failed before. Haho!
   Kings' bones, and gold. Into the sack, all of it. Aeeh, what's
   that noise? Is . . . anybody . . . there? Nothing. Get a nurdle
   on. All of it. You need to see daylight, don't you, cash? Had it
   up to here with tombs? Put back the stone . . . Ah! That
   noise again. I'm scared. I've had enough. I'll come back for
   the rest some other time. Tomorrow.

VOICE *(from the tomb of* STANLEY THE USUALLY SILENT).
   Never, Ma Ubu.

   MA UBU *shrieks and flees through the secret door, lugging the cashsack.*

2 *Square in the capital.* BILLIKINS, CHAPS, SOLDIERS,
PEOPLE.

BILLIKINS. I say, chaps, three cheers for Baloney and Good King
   Wenceslas. That bounder Ubu's legged it. There's no one left
   but Mater Ubu and Big Bad Bernie. I've an idea. Suppose I
   lead you chaps, chuck 'em out and restore my royal race?

ALL. Yay! Billikins! I say!

BILLIKINS. And when we've done that, we'll abolish all the
   taxes imposed by that great oik Ub.

ALL. Hurray! I say! On to the palace. Exterminate!

BILLIKINS. Oh look. Ma Ubu and her guards. There, on the palace steps.

MA UBU. What is it, gents? Oh, Billikins.

The CROWD *throws stones.*

FIRST GUARD. There's not a window left.

SECOND GUARD. They got me. Ah.

THIRD GUARD. I'm done for. Oh.

BILLIKINS. Keep chucking, chaps.

BIG BAD BERNIE. Hoho! Heehee! Haha!

He draws his sword and rushes among them, creating horrible havoc.

BILLIKINS. You swine. On guard.

They fight a duel.

BIG BAD BERNIE. Aah. Eeh. Ooh.

BILLIKINS. I win. Ma Ubu now.

Trumpets sound.

Jolly good. Here come the upper crust. Don't let her get away.

MA UBU *runs away, with all the* BALONIANS *after her. Shots; stones.*

3 *With* UBU's *army, marching in Russkiland.*

PA UBU. Hobblit, daggit, naggit, we're passing out. Curdled. Oi, squaddie, hump this cash-helmet. Sarge, take the clacker-snips, the poky-stick. That's better. I tell you again: our cashness is curdled.

The SOLDIERS *obey.*

WALLOP. Seeyou, pal. Whirthell they Russkies?

PA UBU. It's bloody marvellous. Not enough cash for a chariot that fits. I ask you. To stop the nag knackering under us, our cashness has had to walk. Leading the bleeder. Just wait till we get back to Baloney. Five minutes with our physics set, our poofiprofs, we'll invent a wind-cart to waft us wherever we want. Us and our army. Well?

McCLUB. Sorsor, Nick Nackerley. Sure tis a rush he's in.

PA UBU. All right, all right. What's up?

NICK NACKERLEY. Lord, all is lost. The Balonians have broken out. Big Bad Bernie's dead. Ma Ubu's hiding in the hills.

PA UBU. Polecat! Vulture! Fruitbat! Where did that lot come from? Puddle me. Who's responsible? Billikins, betya. Where have you come from?

NICK NACKERLEY. Baloney, sire.

PA UBU. Shikt, son, if I thought this was true we'd all be on our way home right now. But see here, sonny, you've got cloud for brains. You're dreaming, sonnikins. Go to the front line. Take a look: Russkies. We'll make a sortie, sunshine. Give it all we've got: shikthooks, cashpikes, everything.

GENERAL CUSTARD. Pa Ubu, look. Wusskies.

PA UBU. You're right. Russkies. Brilliant. If we'd some way out of here. But we haven't. We're on a hill; we're sitting ducks.

SOLDIERS. Russkies! Woe! The foe!

PA UBU. Time to get organised. For battle. We'll stay up here. No point in going down there. I'll stand in the middle. Like a living citadel. You can all protect me. Stuff your guns with bullets. Eight bullets means eight dead Russkies, eight more bastards off my back. Light armed Foot, down there. Wait till they charge, then killem. Heavy Horse, hang back, then charge. Artillery here, all round this windmill. If anything moves, shoot it. Me? Us? We'll wait inside the windmill. We'll stick our cashcannon through the window, bar the door with our poky-stick, and if anyone breaks in, they'll be really in the shikt.

OFFICERS. Sah! Sah! Sah!

PA UBU. We'll win, no problem. What time is it?

A cuckoo crows three times.

GENERAL CUSTARD. Eleven a.m.

PA UBU. Dinner time. They'll not attack till twelve. General Laski, tell the men: fall out and pee, then fall back in and start the Cashnal Anthem.

GENERAL CUSTARD. Sah. Weady, chaps? By the wight in thwees. Left wight, left wight.

Exit CUSTARD *and* ARMY. *Impressive orchestral introduction.* PA UBU *sings. The* ARMY *comes back in time to join in the chorus.*

PA UBU. God save our gracious me,
Long live our noble me,
Pour me some –

SOLDIERS. Beer, beer, beer, beer, beer, beer, beer, beer.

PA UBU. Fill up your tanks and then
Unzip your pants and then
All start to –

SOLDIERS. Pee, pee, pee, pee, pee, pee, pee, pee.

PA UBU. Soon as you've room for more
Flap gob and start to pour,
Fill up with –

SOLDIERS. Beer, beer, beer, beer, beer, beer, beer, beer.

PA UBU. I love it. I love you all.

SOLDIERS and BARMPOTS. Till, till, till, till,
Tax, tax, tax, tax,
Up Ubu, up Ubu,
Ting, ting-a-ting.

PA UBU. I love it. I love you all.

A Russkie cannonball flies in and smashes the windmill's sail.

Ahoo! Help! They got me. No, I lied. They didn't.

4 PA UBU, GENERAL CUSTARD, MAJOR F. FORT, TSAR
ALEXIS, DOGPILE, SOLDIERS, BARMPOTS, UBU's ARMY,
RUSSKIE ARMY.

MAJOR F. FORT (*arriving*). Lord Ubu, the Russkies are
attacking.

PA UBU. Don't look at me. Snot my fault. Cashofficers, prepare
for battle.

GENERAL CUSTARD. Another cannon ball.

PA UBU. I'm off. It's raining lead and iron. My cashness could
get seriously croaked. Down the hill.

*They all rush down the hill. Battle has begun. They vanish in the clouds
of smoke at the foot of the hill.*

RUSSKIE (*slashing*). Yah! Take that.

GENERAL CUSTARD. Ouch. That weally hurt.

PA UBU. Say your prayers, pigbreath. Put that down. You don't
scare me.

RUSSKIE. Oh, don't I? Right.

He fires.

PA UBU. Oh! I'm hit, I'm leaking, I'm buried. Only kidding.
Here!

He tears strips off him.

You, Custard. Start again.

GENERAL CUSTARD. Forward. Push. Mark the man, not the ball. We're winning.

PA UBU. You think so? What are these, then? Black eyes, not medals, mate.

RUSSKIE CAVALRYMEN. Make way! His Totality the Tsar.

TSAR ALEXIS *arrives, with* DOGPILE *in disguise.*

BALONIAN SOLDIER. Help! The Tsar.

ANOTHER. He's crossed the ditch.

ANOTHER. Who's that bastard with him? The one with the big sword. Yike! That's four he's sliced.

DOGPILE. Had enough? Want more? Who the hell are you? Ha! Hey! Any more of you?

He massacres Balonians.

PA UBU. Don't just stand there. Grab him. Slab the whole lot of them. We're winning. Up ours!

ALL. Up ours! Godnagit. Grab them. Get that big bastard. Now.

DOGPILE. Sangorge. Ow.

PA UBU (*recognising him*). It's Dogpile. Well, well, well. Have we something nice for you? You like things hot. Cashkindlers, light the fire. Yarg! Ooh! I'm dead. A cannonball. Our favverwichartinevven, forgivmasins. No doubt, a cannonball.

DOGPILE. It was a water pistol.

PA UBU. Bastard. Now you're for it.

He runs at him and tears strips off him.

GENERAL CUSTARD. Lord Ubu, we're winning.

PA UBU. Of course we are. I'm exhausted. I'm black and blue. I've gottosiddown. I'm globbed.

GENERAL CUSTARD. Pa Ubu, it's the Tsar you want to glob.

PA UBU. You're right. Shiktsword, hup! Cashook, ha-hey!

There's work to do. How's my dear little poky-stick? All ready to tsap that Tsar? Ha-ho! Bring Cashnag, my charger, here.

He hurls himself at TSAR ALEXIS.

RUSSKIE OFFICER. Look out, sire!

PA UBU. Go stuff yourself. Ow! What are you doing? Can't we discuss this? I'm sorry, master. Don't be cross. I didn't do it on purpose.

He legs it. TSAR ALEXIS *runs after him.*

Oh shikt, he's after me. He's furious. Oh brilliant, here's the ditch. The ditch in front, and him behind. Nothing for it. Eyes shut and –

He jumps the ditch. TSAR ALEXIS *falls in.*

TSAR ALEXIS . I've fallen in.

POLSKIES. He's ditched! Hurrah!

PA UBU. Hm. Dare I look? He's fallen in. They're bashing his bonce. That's good. Keep at it, lads. Kick him, strangle him, smash the swine. I daren't watch. It's all come out exactly as we predicted. One's poky-stick did sterling work. One would have completely done him in if dire, sudden dread hadn't drained one's deadliness. One was unexpectedly compelled to do a runner. We owe our present safety, in part, to our own imperial skill as horseman and in part to the hocks and withers of our charger Cashnag, whose speed is equalled only by his strength and whose swiftness is sung in song and story – oh and the deepness of the ditch which loomed at the feet of the foe of yourumble serfint chancellstecker. Bloody good speech. Why thangyew. Pity no one else was listening. Back to work!

The Russkie Light Horse make a sortie and rescue TSAR ALEXIS.

GENERAL CUSTARD. We've weally had it now.

PA UBU. I'm off, then. Balonians, quick march. This way. No, that way.

BALONIANS. Run for it!

PA UBU. You said it. Stop pushing. Don't jostle. Make room for me.

He is jostled.

Watch it. Wanna coppa cashclub? He's gone. Right, leg it, and fast before that Laski sees us.

He goes. Soon afterwards, we see TSAR ALEXIS *and the* RUSSKIE ARMY *routing the Balonians.*

5 *Cave in the hills. It is snowing.* PA UBU, WALLOP, McCLUB.

PA UBU. Fweeorg. It's cold. Brass monkeys. My cashness is not enjoying this.

WALLOP. Seeyou, pal. How's the terror? How's the running?

PA UBU. The terror's gone. I've still got the runs.

McCLUB (*aside*). Osor, osor.

PA UBU. Hey McClub. Your snickersnack. Howizzit?

McCLUB. Fine sor, tanksforaskin. Except it's not well at all, atall. I can't get the bullet out. Seesor, it's dragging on the ground.

PA UBU. That'll teach you. Button it up, next time. You want to be like me. Lion-hearted, but cautious. I massacred four of them, in person, not counting the ones that were dead already when I did 'em.

WALLOP. Seeyou, McClub. What happened to wee Nick Nackerley?

McCLUB. Brained by a bullet.

PA UBU. Behold, as the flowers of the field are felled, hoed by the heedless, heartless hoe of the heedless, heartless hoer who heartlessly hacks their heads, so now Nick Nackerley. Proud as a poppy, dead as a dandelion. Fiercely he fought, but there were just too-too many Russkies.

WALLOP. Seeyou.

McCLUB. Sorsor.

ECHO. Ee-oo-aw.

WALLOP. Wossaht? Whairsma-weenife?

PA UBU. Not more Russkies. I'm sick of them. Where are you? I'll blugger the lotayoo.

6   *Enter a* BEAR.

McCLUB. Osor, osor.

PA UBU. Oh look. Nice doggie. Here boy. Miaow, miaow.

WALLOP. Jings, it's a fooky bear, anabigyin.

PA UBU. A bear! A fookybear! It'll eat me. Dog protect me. It's coming for me. No, it's biting McClub. What a relief.

The BEAR *attacks* McCLUB. WALLOP *goes for it with his knife.* UBU *climbs a rock.*

McCLUB. Help. Wallop. Sorsorelp.

PA UBU. Get stuffed. We're saying our prayers. It's you it's eating: not our turn.

WALLOP. Ahavit, Ahavit.

McCLUB. Pull. It's weakening, sohtis.

PA UBU. For wotweerabowtoreseev.

McCLUB. Sorosor.

WALLOP. It's got me in its fangs. Ah hate this.

PA UBU. Thelordsmasheperd.

McCLUB. There. Got it.

WALLOP. It's bleeding. Yay!

In the midst of the BARMPOTS' *cheers, the* BEAR *roars in agony and* PA UBU *continues to mutter prayers.*

McCLUB. Hold it tight. I'll get my nuclear knuckleduster.

PA UBU. Makethmetoliedown.

WALLOP. Hurry up. Ahcannycope.

PA UBU. Greenpasturesleadeathme.

McCLUB. There. Here.

Huge explosion. The BEAR *falls dead.*

WALLOP *and* McCLUB. Ta-RA!

PA UBU. Stillwatersby amen. Well? Is it dead yet? Can I come down off this rock?

WALLOP (*scornfully*). Please yersel.

PA UBU (*climbing down*). Well, aren't you lucky? Still alive, still slushing the snow – and all thanks to my imperial cashness. Who was it who nabbled his nidgets and gabbled his gob saying prayers for you? Who acked it with oliness as bravely as Barmpot McClubere banged it withis brassnuckle bomlet? Who urried up this illere to itch is words igher in eaven's earole?

WALLOP. Yerbum.

PA UBU. What a monster. Thanks to me: dinner. Look at its belly. The Greeks could have used it for a woodenorse. Room for plenty more inside – as we very nearly saw for ourselves, dear friends.

WALLOP. Ma gut thinks ma throat's been cut. What's teat?

McCLUB. Bear.

PA UBU. No, no, no, no, no. Are you going to eat it raw? We've nothing to light a fire.

WALLOP. We've pustols, flunts.

PA UBU. So we have. And now I remember, there's a bunchatrees just up the road, crammed with dry wood. McClub, go fetch.

McCLUB *trudges off across the snow.*

WALLOP. Right. Lord Ubu, you carve.

PA UBU. Ah no. It may not be really dead. In any case, you're half eaten already. Bitten to bits. You do it. I'll light the fire, ready for when he brings the wood.

WALLOP *starts carving up the* BEAR.

Ah! He moved.

WALLOP. Lord Ubu, he's cold.

PA UBU. Tut. So much nicer hot. He'll give my cashness indigestion.

WALLOP (*aside*). He's terrable. (*aloud*) Lord Ubu, give us a hand. Ahcannycope.

PA UBU. I can't. I won't. I'm tired.

McCLUB (*returning*). Snojoke. Snoin. Slike the North Pole, sohtis, or the West Pole. Safter teatime. Lbedark in anhour. Lessgeta move on while we can still see. At all.

PA UBU. Hear that, Wallop? Get on. Both of you, gerron. Carvim, cookim, I'm starvinere.

WALLOP. Seeyou, fatso. Ifye willniwork, yecannyeat.

PA UBU. See if I care. I like it raw. It's you two who'll suffer. I'm going to sleep.

McCLUB. Sleep, is it? Sure and we'll do the job ourselves. He'll not see none of it, willewallop? Praps a bit of a bone or two.

WALLOP. The fire's beginnintaeburn.

PA UBU. That's better. Warmer. Russkies, everywhere. What a victory. Ah.

He falls asleep.

McCLUB. Now, master Wallop, what say you? Nick Nackerley brought news: what truth was in't? The common talk is this: Ma Ubu deposéd stands. In my nostrils, it hath the smell of truth.

WALLOP. Purrameatonablurryfire.

McCLUB. Nay, matters more urgent crave attention. And ere we act, we must have certain news.

WALLOP. Thou hast the right of it. Pa Ubu sleepeth. Shall we leave him where he lieth, or thtay with him?

McCLUB. Night bringeth counsel. Knit up the ravelled sleeve of sleep, and when Dawn's candles prick we'll know just what to do.

WALLOP. Nay. While yet tis dark, snatch our chance and scarper.

McCLUB. After you.

They go.

7

PA UBU (*talking in his sleep*). Russkies, don't shoot. There's some-one here. Whosat? Dogpile. Can't bearim. Bear. As bad as Billikins. He's after me as well. Gerroff. Shoo. Buggeroff. Nick Nackerley, now. The Tsar. Can't touch ME-hee. Missussubu. What you got there, girl? Wheredyoo get that gold? Thass-mine, you old bag, you been diggin in the cathedral. Digginup my tomb. I've been dead for years. Billikins done me in. Laid to rest in the Cathedral. Next to Vaslav the Versatile. And in the cemetery, next to Roger the Ratbag. And in that prison cell, next to Dogpile. Not him again. Bear, buggeroff. Satanspawn, begawn. What d'you mean, can't hear me? Oh, the Barmpots lopped your lugoils. Debrainin, snackersnikin, taxnabbin, boozinanboozin, thassalife. For Barmpots, Cashlads, his right royal cashness, me.

He snores and sleeps.

End of Act Four.

Act Five

1 *Night.* PA UBU *asleep.* MA UBU *comes in. She doesn't see him. It's pitch dark.*

MA UBU. At last, somewhere to hide. No one about. Suits me. What a journey! Four days; one end of Baloney to the other. Whatever *could* have happened, *happened*, all at once. Fatso nags out of it on his charger. I creep into the crypt to nabisloot. Next thing, Billikins and his berserkers are almost stoning me to death. I lose my protector, Big Bad Bernie, who was so besotted with my charms that he fell in a heap every time he saw me, and every time he didn't, which is a sign of real true love. Said he'd be sliced into snippets for my sake, poor lamb. And so he was. By Billikins. Slish, slash, slosh. Aah. I nearly died. Anyway, I escape. They're all after me. Foaming with fury. I leave the palace. Down to the river. Guards on every bridge. I swim across: that'll foolem. Nobs pile after me. I'm surrounded, on every side. They're foaming at the mouth. At last I make it. One end of Baloney to the other. Four days, tramping through the snow in my own queendom, as used to be, till I end up here. Safe. Four days, I haven't et or drunk. Billikins was too close for that. Nehmind, I made it. Bleah, I'm famished. I'm freezing. What happened to old lardibags, I mean to my lord and master? Not to mention Cashnag. Died of hunger, poor old devil. Nehmind, eh? *And* I forgot the treasure. Left it in the palace. Finders keepers. Who cares?

PA UBU (*stirring in his sleep*). Arrest Ma Ubu. Snackersnicker.

MA UBU. Aee. Where is this? I don't believe it. Dog, no! Pa Ubu sleepineer? That's queer. Wake him gently. Oi, gutbag, shake a leg.

PA UBU. Bloodyell, didyeseet? That bear? It was brain against bruin. Brian won, completely gobbled and globbed that brown. Wait till it's light, lads: you'll see, you'll see.

MA UBU. He's babbling. Dafter than when he started. Who's he on about?

PA UBU. McClub! Wallop! Sakashikt, where are you? I'm scared. Someone said something. Who? Not . . . the bear? Shikt. Matches, matches . . . Lostem in the fight.

MA UBU (*aside*). Exploit the state he's in, the dark. Pretend to be a spook. Make him promise to forgiveusour cashpassin.

PA UBU. Dogalmighty. There is someone there. O-elp. I wish I was dead.

MA UBU (*making her voice huge*). True, Ubu, too troo. There's someone here. The voice of doom looms from the tomb. Your fairy godmother: speciality, good advice.

PA UBU. Get stuffed.

MA UBU. Interrupt me not, or I shut my gob and you get stuffed.

PA UBU. Cornswobbit. Not another word. Do go on, your spookiness.

MA UBU. We were just going to say, Master Ubu, what a naughty little boy you are.

PA UBU. Naughty. What? Yes. Yes.

MA UBU. Godnagit, shuttit!

PA UBU. A swearing fairy.

MA UBU (*aside*). Shikt. (*aloud*) Master Ub, you're married?

PA UBU. To vinegar-features, of course I am.

MA UBU. You mean, to the most charming waife in all the world.

PA UBU. I mean, a porcupine. Prickles everywhere. You don't know where to grab.

MA UBU. Try grabbing naicely. She could be ever so naice.

PA UBU. So full of lice?

MA UBU. Listen! Willy little boy! Sit up straight, fold your arms, pay attention! (*aside*) Get a nurdle on. It's nearly dawn. (*aloud*) Master Ub, your waife is soft and sweet, without a fault.

PA UBU. Ah, rubbish. It's *all* her fault.

MA UBU. Dognagit. She's true to you, too troo.

PA UBU. Of course she is. Who else'd have her?

MA UBU. Bastard! (*recovering*) Your waife steals not your gold.

PA UBU. Rubbish.

MA UBU. Not a penny peeeece.

PA UBU. So wottabat dear ole Cashnag? Three months, nothing teat, dragged by the bridle halfway round the world, dead in harness, poor old devil.

MA UBU. Not troo! Your waife is sweeeet and you're a beeeest.

PA UBU. Stuff yoo! My wife's a tart and you're a fart.

MA UBU. Master Ub, beware. You murdered Good King Wenceslas.

PA UBU. Not my fault. Ma Ubu made me.

MA UBU. You had Willy and Silly done to death.

PA UBU. Tough titty. They were after me.

MA UBU. You broke your word to Dogpile. Then you killed him.

PA UBU. He wanted to be Lord de Lawdy. So did I. Now no one is. That proves it. It wasn't me.

MA UBU. There's only one way to redeeeem your siiiiiins.

PA UBU. What is it? I'll do anything, be good, be nice, be famous.

MA UBU. You must forgive Ma Ubu for snafflin a bit of snitch.

PA UBU. Forgive her, yes. When she pays it back, when I blattererer blackanbloo, when she gives ole Cashnag the kissolife.

MA UBU. He's hooked on that horse. Yike, I'm done for: dawn.

PA UBU. So now I've proof, my own missus was robbinme. You told me. She's additnow. Guilty as charged, verdict of you all, hanged by the neck, signed, sealed delivered, no appeal. Hey up: dawn. Cashnagit, it's her. Ma Ubu.

MA UBU (*offendedly*). Coursitsnot. I'll doooo for yoooo.

PA UBU. Come off it, nagbag.

MA UBU. Cheeky devil.

PA UBU. I can see it's you. What the L U doinere?

MA UBU. Big Bad Bernie's dead and the Balonians are after me.

PA UBU. Thassalaff. The Russkies a rafterME. And when they catch me –

MA UBU. They can keep you.

PA UBU. They can keep this fookybear. Here, catch.

He throws the BEAR *at her.*

MA UBU (*collapsing under it*). Ai. Yarg. Bleah. I can't breathe. It's biting me. It's eating me. It's digesting me.

PA UBU. It's dead, you fool. Just a minute, spose-it snot? Salive? O-eck.

He climbs his rock again.

Our fetherwich artineven.

MA UBU (*throwing off the* BEAR). Where's he gone?

PA UBU. Yike. She'sere! Protectusfromevil. Is it dead?

MA UBU. It's all right, ploppipants, it's cold. How did it get here?

PA UBU (*mumbling*). I dunno. Yes I do. It was going to eat Wallop and McClub, but I killed it with a pilaprayer.

MA UBU. Wallop, McClub, a pilaprayer? Cashnagit, he's off his nut.

PA UBU. *You*'re off *your* nut, naggybag.

MA UBU. So tell me about your fighting.

PA UBU. Won't. Too long. I was very, very brave, and they all kept hitting me.

MA UBU. Even the Balonians?

PA UBU. 'Up Wence!' they shouted. 'Up Billikins!' They were really after me. And they crushed poorole Custard.

MA UBU. See if I care. Billikins bashed up Big Bad Bernie.

PA UBU. See if I care. They knackered Nick Nackerley.

MA UBU. See if I care.

PA UBU. Right, naggybag, that does it. Cumere. Down on thy knees, avaunt.

He forces her to her knees.

Base wretch, thou'rt for it now.

MA UBU. You and whose army?

PA UBU. Denosing, deluggering, debumming, debraining, demarrowing, deswimbladdering, deneckeration. Whaddyoo thinkoTHIS?

He tears strips off her.

MA UBU. Ow. Pa Ubu. No.

Huge noise outside the cave.

2 PA UBU, MA UBU, BILLIKINS, CHAPS.

BILLIKINS *and his* CHAPS *rush into the cave.*

BILLIKINS. This way, chaps. Yay! Up Baloney!

PA UBU. Hang on, I'm busy. My better half.

BILLIKINS (*bashing him*). Take that, you pig, you dog, you louse, you chicken, you unmitigated swine.

PA UBU (*giving as good as he gets*). Take that, pintpot, poultice, salad-bowl, squirt, stuffed shirt.

MA UBU (*having a bash as well*). Take that, babyface, pisspant, noserag, bumwipe, bib.

The CHAPS *pile on. The* UBS *defend themselves as best they can.*

PA UBU. There's millions of em.

MA UBU. So kick their heads in.

PA UBU. Stagger me sideways, yes. Haha, haHA. Another one! I wish I'd Cashnag ere.

BILLIKINS. Bashem. On! On! On!

VOICE (*off*). Up Ubu. His Cashness. Yaaah!

PA UBU. At last. The Ubbibums. This way, cashhounds, eel, inere.

The BARMPOTS *pile in and pile on.*

McCLUB. Start runnin, Balonians, sotis, yaah.

WALLOP. Seeyooboo, pushyerweewayoot. Taethedoor. Then run.

BILLIKINS. I say. That hurt.

BARMPOT. No it didn't.

BILLIKINS. Oh, right. Willy me.

ANOTHER BARMPOT. They're nearly out. On, on, on, on.

WALLOP. Thisway. Ahcanseeablurrysky. CumOHN.

McCLUB. Osor, don't panic. Run.

PA UBU. Now I've flapped in my pants. Cornswobbit, NOW!
Bangem, blobem, gashem, globem. HaHAH.

WALLOP. Two left. Behind you. There.

PA UBU (*bashing them with the* BEAR). One, two. Feeoo! There!
I'm out. Run for it. This way. After meeeeeeee!

3 *The Middle of Nowhere. It's snowy.* THE UBS *and the*
BARMPOTS, *legging it.*

PA UBU. We've made it. They've given up.

MA UBU. He's gone to be crowned, that Billikins.

PA UBU. He can keep his crown.

MA UBU. Pa Ubu, you're right.

They disappear into the distance.

4 *On board a ship skimming the ocean. On deck,* PA UBU *and all
the rest.*

CAPTAIN. What a balmy breeze.

PA UBU. Observe with what prodigious speed we skim the
waves. At a rough estimate, one million knots per hour. Reef
knots, every one of them. It's what we sailors call a breeze
behind.

WALLOP. Blowtoot yerbum.

Sudden squall. The ship yaws.

PA UBU. Yike. Eee. We're done for. We're sinking. We're drowning. It's your fault. It's your boat.

CAPTAIN. All hands to the forestopspritsal. Chocks away.

PA UBU. Idiot. Stackinussall thisside. What if the wind changes? We'll fall in. Fishll finishuss.

CAPTAIN. Luff the portcullis. Steady Eddy.

PA UBU. Stuff steady. Get a nurdle on. I want to get there. If we never get there, it'll be all your fault. We've got to get there. Oh here, let me. Splice the mainbrace. Any more for the skylark? Keelhaul the binnacle. Mr Christian, avast behind. What? What?

All scream with laughter. The wind rises.

CAPTAIN. Break out the pipsal and pass to port.

PA UBU. You eardim, pass the port.

They're kicking their legs in the air with laughing. A wave hits the ship.

Hey, that was a biggun. We know what we're doing.

MA UBU, WALLOP. Lovely day for a cruise.

A second wave hits the ship.

WALLOP (*soaked*). Seeyou, repent or die.

PA UBU. Waiter! Oi, waiter! A drop to drink.

They all settle down to drink.

MA UBU. How naice to visit Engelland once more. One's favourite little country. One's hice in the highlands. One's dear old friends.

PA UBU. Not far now. Just passing Germany.

WALLOP. Jings, ahcannywait taeseemaweeWales.

McCLUB. Sure and aren't they the tales we'll have to tell?

PA UBU. Firstoff, I'm off to London. His Cashness Prince of the Piggybank.

MA UBU. How naice. Ow what ai waive.

McCLUB. Twas the Dogger Bank, suretwas.

WALLOP. Seejimmy thileaskye.

PA UBU. They call it the Isle of Sky because it's blue.

MA UBU. Pa Ubu, you know everything.

PA UBU. Course I do. Swot got me ere ina firstplace.

The End.

CUCKOLD UBU

Characters

PA UBU
HIS CONSCIENCE
MA UBU
PEARDROP
FLUNKEY
BARMPOT BUMRAG
NARMPOT SNOTWEED
BARMPOT GRIPSHIT
MEMNON
SWANKIPANTS THE BANKER
BOBBLER THE COBBLER

Act One

1   PEARDROP.

PEARDROP. What, me dissatisfied? With my polyhedrons? Ooh *no*, snark. They produce little polyhedrons every six weeks, worse than rabbits. They're very affectionate, the regular polyhedrons especially. Understand every word I say. The icosahedron *was* a bit naughty this morning, needed a smack on the botty, well, all twenty botties. But they like a firm hand, snark. I'm writing a thesis all about them. Coming on nicely. Only twenty-five volumes to go.

2   PEARDROP, FLUNKEY.

FLUNKEY. Bloke at the door. Wantsta talkteryer. Tore aht the bell, pullinit. Smashed free chairs, sittin dahninem.

He hands him a visiting card.

PEARDROP. Whatever does it mean? 'Monsieur Ubu, ex-king of Baloney, Doctor of Pataphysics.' He's lost me there. Pataphysics, snark. Never mind, he's obviously important. I'll show him my polyhedrons. Show the gentleman in.

3   PEARDROP, UBU (*dressed for a journey, carrying a suitcase*).

UBU. Stagger me sideways, mate, this placeayours is rubbish. I was ringin that bell for an hour. An when they *did* open the door, it was so small my gurdlenacker nearly knotted itself gettin through.

PEARDROP. Sorry, snark. We don't get visitors your size. If I'd known, I'd have got a bigger door. So sorry. You'll have to excuse me. Absent-minded old professor, snark. Expert in the field.

UBU. Nehmind *your* field. *Mine's* pataphysics.

PEARDROP. Excuse me?

PA UBU. Pataphysics. The world was cryin out for it, so I invented it.

PEARDROP. An inventor. Pleased to meet you. We'll get on *so* well: great minds, snark.

PA UBU. Oojoo think you are? There's only one mindere, that's mine. Still, nehmind. I've decided to bless your umbleome. It suits us. We're movin in.

PEARDROP. I'm sorry, snark . . .

PA UBU. No, don't thank me. The wifenkidsll be ere any minute. Ma Ubu, the Ublets. They're serious people, they been to school.

PEARDROP. You don't understand. Snark. I'm afraid . . .

PA UBU. You're afraid you'll be in the way. Don't worry, if you are we'll tell you. Now, I want to see the kitchen, the dining room. You'll find three trunks outside the door. Fetchemin.

PEARDROP. Taking over someone else's house. It's . . . snark, it's unbelievable.

PA UBU. Yer. Well. Hop, hop, hop.

Exit PEARDROP.

4   PA UBU, HIS CONSCIENCE.

PA UBU. Should we have done that? Stagger me sideways,
   cornswobbit, I'll ask my conscience. Sere, in the suitcase.
   Fwah, cobwebs. Dunt get out much.

He opens the suitcase, and his CONSCIENCE *comes out. It's tall,
thin, in a nightshirt.*

CONSCIENCE. Dear Enquirer, etc. You may take this down.

PA UBU. Hang on: writin. I don't do writin. Even if what you
   say *is* intrestin. Who said you could come outere in your
   nightshirt?

CONSCIENCE. Dear Enquirer, etc. Conscience, like Truth, goes
   normally unclad. If I wear a nightshirt, it's because of these
   lazangennelmen.

PA UBU. That's enough messing. Answer a question. This bloke
   Peardrop, insulted me in my own front room. Am I right to
   killim?

CONSCIENCE. Dear Enquirer, etc. Two rights don't make a
   wrong. Monsieur Peardrop took you in. He opened his arms
   (and his collection of polyhedrons) to welcome you. Etc, etc.
   He's done you no harm, he can't protect himself, only a
   coward would kill him. Yours, etc.

PA UBU. Stagger me sideways, he can't protect himself?

CONSCIENCE. Enquirer, no. That's why only a coward would
   kill him.

PA UBU. Thanks. Go back to sleep. I'll kill him, since he won't
   fight back, and I'll talk to you again, often. I like your advice.
   In you go!

He shuts it back in the suitcase.

CONSCIENCE. That's all we have time for. In tomorrow's
   session we'll . . .

5   PA UBU, PEARDROP, FLUNKEY.

PEARDROP *scrabbles in backwards, pursued by three red trunks pushed by the* FLUNKEY.

PA UBU (*to the* FLUNKEY). Right, you, nagit. An *you*, I want you to do somethin.

PEARDROP. Anything, snark. Just remember I *am* a polyhedron specialist, sixty years I've spent with them, they're all I know.

PA UBU. A lilbird's just tole me, Ma Ubu my ballanchain's been avinitoff with some Egyptian. Memnon is nameis. Sings at dawn every mornin, empties sewage tanks all night, asitaway all day with Ma Ubu. 'E's mine. I'll avim. Stagger me sideways, 'e woneven *know* wot itim.

PEARDROP. That's very sad. Having it off with your wife. How sad.

PA UBU. Sad for *im*. What'm I plannin forim? Stake up the bum.

PEARDROP. Ah. Yes. I don't quite see . . . Where do I come in?

PA UBU. Stagger me sideways, I aveto practise.

PEARDROP. Ah. Snark. No, I'm sorry. I won't. I simply won't. You nick my house, you throw me out, and now you want to kill me. Oh no, snark, no.

PA UBU. Keep your nurdles on. Only jokin. Calm down, an *then* we'll talk.

Exit.

6   PEARDROP, BARMPOTS.

The three BARMPOTS *come out of the trunks.*

BARMPOTS.
>Ooah ooah ooah,
>Barmpots are out,
>Yell, scream an shout,
>Ooah ooah ooah.

BUMRAG.
>All week it's borin.
>We lie there snorin.
>Then Satdi comes.
>You askin for trouble?
>We'll give you trouble,
>When Satdi comes.

BARMPOTS.
>Ooah ooah ooah,
>Barmpots are out,
>Yell, scream an shout,
>Ooah ooah ooah.

SNOTWEED.
>Ubu's our leader,
>We love the bleeder
>When Satdi comes.
>You lookin at mepal?
>You better not bepal,
>When Satdi comes.

They dance. PEARDROP, *terrified, slumps in a chair.*

BARMPOTS.
>Ooah ooah ooah,
>Barmpots are out,
>Yell, scream an shout,
>Ooah ooah ooah.

GRIPSHIT.
>Youread needs shattrin,
>Yourbum needs battrin
>When Satdi comes?
>You think you're well hard, mate?

You come with a guard, mate,
When Satdi comes.

BARMPOTS.
Ooah ooah ooah,
Barmpots are out,
Yell, scream an shout,
Ooah ooah ooah.

They dance round PEARDROP.

PEARDROP. You'd better stop this. Snark. It's ridiculous. It's *surreal*.

The stake begins to rise beneath his chair.

It's *unheard* of. If you were *polyhedrons* . . . I'm an old man . . .
A man of science . . . What're you doing? It isn't *fair*.

He is impaled high in the air, for all his shrieks. Blackout.

BARMPOTS (*pulling the furniture apart and grabbing bags of cash*).
Cash, cash, cash, cash.
Pa Ubu's cash.
Find it, find, it, find it.
Cash, cash, cash, cash,
Pa Ubu's lovely cash.

They get back inside their trunks.

Ooah ooah ooah,
Barmpots are out,
Yell, scream an shout,
Ooah ooah ooah.

PEARDROP *faints.*

7   PEARDROP *on his stake*, PA UBU, MA UBU.

PA UBU. Stagger me sideways, gel, we'll like it ere.

MA UBU. Very naice. I'd laike to meet our generous host.

PA UBU. Easy. Up there, on the seat of honour.

He shows her the stake. Shriekin and cryin from MA UBU.

End of Act One.

Act Two

1 PEARDROP *impaled.* Ubu's CONSCIENCE, *half out of its suitcase.*

CONSCIENCE. Dear Enquirer.

PEARDROP. Fffffffreep.

CONSCIENCE. Etc.

PEARDROP. No, no, fffffffreeep, snark. I'm supposed to be dead. Leave me alone.

CONSCIENCE. Dear Enquirer, Although my conditions of employment forbid direct action, I'm so outraged at what Monsieur Ubu's done, I'm going to unstake you.

It stretches itself as high as PEARDROP.

PEARDROP (*unstaked*). Thanks. Snark.

CONSCIENCE. Dear Enquirer, etc, a moment. Please do sit down.

PEARDROP. Ah, snark, I'd rather not. It would be rude, after all you've done for me, and it'd be uncomfortable.

CONSCIENCE. My voices are telling me, not to mention justice demands, that I punish Monsieur Ubu. Any suggestions?

PEARDROP. Funny you should say that, snark. I've been thinking about it. I'll open the trapdoor to the sewage tank. Put the armchair on the brink. Then when His Fatness sits down after dinner, snargffft!

CONSCIENCE. Justice will be done, and not a moment too soon.

2   PEARDROP, PA UBU.

When PA UBU *comes in, his* CONSCIENCE *hides in its suitcase.*

PA UBU. Stagger me sideways, you've moved. Since you're still useful, tell your cook there was too much salt in the soup and the roast was burnt. Not good. We could use pataphysics to produce banquets, if we wanted. Stuff that, though. It's what goes on in your house, gets right up our nose.

PEARDROP. Snark. Won't trouble you again.

He tips him into the hatch.

See? Snark.

PA UBU. What are you playing at? Your floor's a disgrace. You'll be sorry for this.

PEARDROP. It's a trapdoor, for chrissake.

CONSCIENCE. His Fatness is stuck.

PA UBU. Stagger me sideways, a trapdoor should be shut or it should be open. When you go to the Cashnal Theatre, you expect trapdoors that work. This one's noddlinus, nurkinuss, stiflinourstickersnick. Pullus out or we've adit.

PEARDROP. Terribly sorry. All I can do is soothe your dying ears by reading some choice paragraphs, snark, from my work on polyhedrons. Sixty years I've spent on the ploppipot syndrome alone. No? Snark. I'm off then. Can't bear to watch. It's far too sad.

Exit.

3   PA UBU, CONSCIENCE.

PA UBU. Conscience. Where are you? Stagger me sideways, you were right all the time. We'll do it. Payemallback, shut down the debrainin. Anything.

CONSCIENCE. Dear Enquirer, when a sinner repenteth, etc, etc. I'll help you.

PA UBU. Get a nurdle on. I'm dyinere. Dragusout, and you can stay out of the suitcase till mornin.

The CONSCIENCE *sets him free, and chucks the suitcase down the sewageole.*

CONSCIENCE (*bowing and scraping*). Thankyou, Monsieur. Did you know, Monsieur, gymnastics are good for you. Ask anyone.

PA UBU. Stagger me sideways, you're pulling our leg. *We* do gym. We do it bettrnyoo, too. Watch – an this isn't easy, with a gurdlenacker the sizeo thissun.

He jumps and runs.

CONSCIENCE. Monsieur, don't do that. You'll go through the floor. Now then, watch this.

It hangs up by its feet.

Hang about, I'm stuck. My snackets are stretchin. Pa Ubu, help.

PA UBU (*sitting*). No chance. Digestin our dindins. If we grobbed our gurdlenacker elpinyoo, it could be serious. Two hours, two'nafpraps, we'll lendand. In any case, we don't believe in unookin ookinobs.

The CONSCIENCE *wriggles about and falls on* PA UBU's *gurdlenacker.*

Yike. That's it. You've done it now.

He looks for the suitcase, can't find it, and stuffs the CONSCIENCE *down the sewageole.*

4   PA UBU, BARMPOTS *standing up in their trunks.*

BARMPOTS.
> His girdlenack
> 'Sgreatbigwhack,
> Don't mockit
> Or knockit
> Or 'e'll give you the chop.
> Snot fooey, 'strooey,
> 'E'll give you the chop.

> PA UBU, *meanwhile, has lit his green candles, with their stink of sulphur and the note they sing. He's hung up two notices:* 'Nacknoodlin' *and* 'Tattooin wileyoowate'.

BUMRAG. Sgoinwell, Pa Ubu. One bastard ad *eleven* goes at noodlenackerin this mornin. Hapyoo.

SNOTWEED. Pa Ubu, I delivered the nuclear bomlets to the address you toleme, and the crockshikt to the other address you toleme. Hapyoo.

GRIPSHIT. Pa Ubu, I beenin Egypt. BrungbackMemnon. Singinthing. Tried ter windinimup. Dinwork. Stuckiminacashbox. Hapyoo.

PA UBU. Shurrup the lotayoo. Time for big thinkin. The sphere is a perfect shape. The Sun is a heavenly body. The head in mortals is perfection, oriented always to the Sun and taking its physical form. Only excelled by the eye, which mirrors that heavenly body and taketh shape from it. The sphere is the form of an angel. Mortal form is a poor simulacrum of angelic form: more perfect than the cylinder, less perfect than the sphere. As a barrel radiates hyperphysical matter, so we, its isomorph, are beautiful.

BARMPOTS.
> His girdlenack
> 'Sgreatbigwhack,
> Don't mockit
> Or knockit
> Or 'e'll give you the chop.

PA UBU. Wasn't it Seneca who said, '*Non cum vacaveris, pataphysicandum est*'? In the knitted weave of our philosophy, we must patch and mend. *Omnia alia neglegenda sunt.* Is it not a form of blasphemy, *ut huic assideamus*, employing barrels and buckets for emptyin sacksashikt? Chancellorstecker, one does apologise. *Cui nullum tempus vitae satis magnum est.* With this in mind, we've invented the following apparatus, which we give the utilitarian but not unsatisfying name of Shiktpump.

He takes it from his pocket and puts it on the table.

BARMPOTS. Pa Ooboo, hapyoo.

PA UBU. It's getting late. Time for bed. Oh, by the way, talking of Egypt, we need mummygrease for the machine. Seems it runs too fast, too fast to catch at any rate.

He takes his machine and a green candle and exit.

5   BARMPOTS, MEMNON.

The BARMPOTS *sing in their trunks, while the statue of* MEMNON *rises up in the middle of the floor, supported on a barrel.*

BARMPOTS.
Hey, middle classes, weep and wail,
Our Chancellorstecker praise and hail,
When he clobbers you, when he slobbers you.

Pa Ubu rules, he says wot's wot,
He'll stir the pot and make it hot
Then he'll clobber you, then 'e'll slobber you.

Gets outo bed, Lord fartipants,
He'll nacker you, you won't stand a chance,
When he clobbers you, when he slobbers you.

Lord Ubu, shiktlord, great and grand,
Walked all the way to Russkiland,
An'e'll clobber you, then 'e'll slobber you.

End of Act Two.

Act Three

1   BARMPOTS, *marching.*

BARMPOTS.
Hoo hoo hoo
We're after you.

Are you middle class? Wear a suit? Big office? White face,
brown nose? We're after you.

We'll have your brains for breakfast, your lungs for lunch,
your dingledang for dinner. We're after you.

Hoo hoo hoo
We're after you.

Exeunt.

2   SWANKIPANTS THE BANKER, PEARDROP.

They appear from opposite sides of the stage. SWANKIPANTS THE
BANKER *is dressed in all the gear. The first two speeches are
simultaneous.*

SWANKIPANTS THE BANKER. It's absy outrageous. A simple
accountant, yah? Six hundred K plus benefits, and Ub takes
800 K commission. Pay up or go to the Fat Cat Clinic. A
billion a session. Abslute nightmare, yah?

PEARDROP. It's my house, snark, and it snot my house. Pa
Ubu's made that *very* clear. Booted me out, hasn't he? Not to

mention the – excuse me – shiktpump he's set up in the bedroom. *My* bedroom, snark. Wah! A Barmpot. Arg!

SWANKIPANTS THE BANKER. A Barmpot. Brown-nosim. I say, Pa Ubu's absy one of us.

PEARDROP. He'll stake me if I don't say yes. Yes, yes, nose-nakring, yes. Snark.

SWANKIPANTS THE BANKER. Down with Fat Cats. Brainem.

PEARDROP. You mean, Stakem.

They go towards each other.

SWANKIPANTS THE BANKER. He's coming this way. Dogelpme.

PEARDROP. Frrrrreep. Oelp.

They rush to get away, and bang into each other. PEARDROP *on his knees for mercy.*

Don't Barmpot me. I'm sorry, snark. Dint do it on purpose. I *love* Pa Ubu.

SWANKIPANTS THE BANKER. Don't be ridiculous. *I* love Pa Ubu.

PEARDROP. You're not . . . by any chance . . . I mean . . . a master (snark) sword-fighter?

SWANKIPANTS THE BANKER. Don't be ridiculous.

PEARDROP. Thing is, snark, if you *aren't* a master sword-fighter, here's my card. A duel.

SWANKIPANTS THE BANKER. OK, yah. I lied. I *am* a master sword-fighter.

PEARDROP. In that case . . .

He slaps him.

Give me your card. No, please. I always slap master sword-fighters. They give me their cards. Then I give the cards to

people who *aren't* master sword-fighters so they think *I'm* a
master sword-fighter, but I'm not, I'm really a pacifist, snark.

SWANKIPANTS THE BANKER. Absy outragcous. Waste of
time, anyway. We won't fight a duel. Clear blue water. Not a
level playing field.

PEARDROP. It's all right, I wouldn't hurt you, honest.

A CASHHOUND *crosses the stage.*

SWANKIPANTS THE BANKER. Yike! Did you see that? Pa
Ub sent it. It's globbed my trousers.

PEARDROP. And your shoes. Oh, shame. I was going to ask
you to run away with me.

SWANKIPANTS THE BANKER. I say, where to?

PEARDROP. Somewhere to fight a duel. Far away from Ub.

SWANKIPANTS THE BANKER. Like Brussels, yah?

PEARDROP. Egypt. I need a pyramid, for my collection. We'll
call at Bobbler the Cobbler's on the way, on the corner on
the way, and get you new shoes.

3   SWANKIPANTS THE BANKER, BARMPOTS, MEMNON
on his barrel.

SWANKIPANTS THE BANKER *goes to sit down, as the sun begins
to rise and* MEMNON *begins to play his flute.* SWANKIPANTS
THE BANKER *listens in horror to what follows, but is hidden by the
barrel from the* BARMPOTS, *who enter from the other side.*

MEMNON.
  When I was young I lived round ere, I lived ere with the
      missus,
  And she sewed all the dressing-gowns and I washed all the
      dishes,
  And on Sunday, every Sunday, sunny Sunday, snow or rainin,

We went down to the prison-yard to watch the free debrainin.
Quicky, quicky, slurpitout,
Sicky, sicky, burpitout.

BARMPOTS.
Ubu, Ubu, Ubu-Ubu-Ubu.

MEMNON.
We took our little girlies in their little Sunday frockies,
Red ribbons in their curlies and their pretty Sunday sockies,
And they jumped and clapped their handies, waved their little
    dollies
While they watched the free debrainin and it gave them great
    big jollies.
Quicky, quicky, slurpitout,
Sicky, sicky, burpitout.

BARMPOTS.
Ubu, Ubu, Ubu-Ubu-Ubu.

MEMNON.
We're slashin there in bloodanguts, the brains are
    flopanploppin,
The puddles on the cobbles and the slushpile slippysloppin,
An then I see this bloke I know, e's linin up for boppin,
There's a Barmpot with a napperslice all lifted up for choppin.
Quicky, quicky, slurpitout,
Sicky, sicky, burpitout.

BARMPOTS.
Ubu, Ubu, Ubu-Ubu-Ubu.

MEMNON.
I jumpanshout and screamanshriek, but no one hears me
    yellin.
I glob a dogpile, ripe an new, an fruity, fat and smellin,
I barm that Barmpot's gob, is mateys glob an glab me,
They snaggle off my snickersnack and flib and flob and
    flab me.
Quicky, quicky, slurpitout,
Sicky, sicky, burpitout.

BARMPOTS.
    Ubu, Ubu, Ubu-Ubu-Ubu.

MEMNON.
    The moral of this story is, you wanna funday Sunday,
    You wanna keep your wifeankids, you wanna live till Monday,
    You like your little nickernack, your noddle's not for offin,
    Don't watch debrainin apnin, or you'll end up in a coffin.
    Quicky, quicky, slurpitout,
    Sicky, sicky, burpitout.

BARMPOTS.
    Ubu, Ubu, Ubu-Ubu-Ubu.

4   MEMNON, PEARDROP, BOBBLER THE COBBLER.

The BARMPOTS *get back in their trunks as the sun rises higher.*
PEARDROP *arrives with* BOBBLER THE COBBLER.
BOBBLER THE COBBLER *has a sign with him, and a selection
of shoes on a stand.*

PEARDROP. We *couldn't* come to you. Why not? The unity of
    place. *You* have to come to *us*. Set up shop in here . . .

    He ushers him into the bog.

    Put your sign on the door, and my young friend'll be your
    first customer.

SWANKIPANTS THE BANKER. Learned sir, I was nagging it
    to Egypt with my gentleman friend Peardrop, when a
    Cashhound snaffled my snidgits and snagdem. I beg you,
    therefore, shoe me.

BOBBLER THE COBBLER. Monsieur. May I recommend,
    the dish of the day, in fact the speciality of the house:
    Shiktcrushers? As Monsieur will know, there are all kinds of
    shikt – and there are Shiktcrushers to suit every taste.

Steamheap pressers, Horsepile Honkers, Cowpat blatters, Babyshikt slipslops, Famlimanflanners, and our *pièce de résistance*, we're very proud of these, our range of Copcrapcrushers.

SWANKIPANTS THE BANKER. Yah. These. Make me a deal.

BOBBLER THE COBBLER. Fort-titty pee, that's with full discount, such a valued customer.

PEARDROP. You should have had these. Copcrappercrushers, much more *you*.

SWANKIPANTS THE BANKER. You're absy right. Yah, I'll have these instead.

He starts to leave.

BOBBLER THE COBBLER. Hang on, Sir *is* going to pay?

SWANKIPANTS THE BANKER. You don't do exchanges? I traded that other pair.

BOBBLER THE COBBLER. You didn't pay for those either.

PEARDROP. That's because he didn't take them.

BOBBLER THE COBBLER. Oh yes.

PEARDROP (*to* SWANKIPANTS THE BANKER). It's an old trick, but he's an old cobbler, snark. He'll unload em.

PEARDROP *and* SWANKIPANTS THE BANKER, *on their way out, find themselves face to face with the* BARMPOTS.

5   SWANKIPANTS THE BANKER, PEARDROP, BOBBLER THE COBBLER, BARMPOTS.

BARMPOTS.
   His girdleknack
   'Sgreatbigwhack,

Don't mockit
Or knockit . . .

BUMRAG. Get a nurdle on. Sun's cominup. We have to get inside.

SNOTWEED. 'Ere's wun. Stuffiminatrunk.

GRIPSHIT. Gotcha, dogbreath. Pa Ubu's gonna luvthis.

PEARDROP. You can't do this. Put me down. Don't you recognise me? Snark. Monsieur Peardrop. I've been staked before already.

SWANKIPANTS THE BANKER. Yah, chappie, put me down. This is well out of order. Plus I'm on my way to the Fat Cat Clinic. OK?

SNOTWEED. Wottabiggun.

GRIPSHIT. Legginit.

Fight.

SWANKIPANTS THE BANKER. Help! Bobbler the Cobbler! I'll pay for the shoes.

PEARDROP. Hit them, bash them, beat them.

BOBBLER THE COBBLER. I'm naggin outofere.

A BARMPOT sets his hair on fire.

Yike! My hair, snot fair.

BARMPOTS.
Don't mockit
Or knockit
Or 'e'll give you the chop.

They barbecue BOBBLER THE COBBLER, then shut the bog door on him. A whoosh of flame shoots through the window. They nag MEMNON off his barrel, stuff SWANKIPANTS THE BANKER and PEARDROP into it and nurdle off.

BARMPOTS.
> Cashhounds, cashhounds, nah nahdy nah,
> Bankerswankers, blah blahdy blah,
> We itanit and bashanbash,
> Don't swankit, bankers, we want your cash.

End of Act Three.

Act Four

1   MEMNON, MA UBU.

MEMNON *picks himself up, adjusts his sausage-knotter's hat and his crapwader's bigboots, then opens the door to* MA UBU.

MEMNON. This way, darlin, there's no one ere.

MA UBU. I was so frightened. What they were *doin* to you.

MEMNON. I miss that barrel.

MA UBU. I don't miss Pa Ubu.

MEMNON. Hang about. There's people 'ere. Watchinus. Hide upere.

They move upstage.

2   MEMNON, MA UBU *onstage.* PA UBU, BARMPOTS, *offstage.*

PA UBU (*off*). Stagger me sideways, we nabbed ishouse and grabbed iscash, we stuckimona stake, now our conscience nags us, we wanna findim and givim backis dinner. All overim. Bleah.

BARMPOTS (*off*).
   Snot fooey, strooey,
   'E'll give you the chop.

MA UBU. It's Pa Ubu. I'm done for.

MEMNON. His cashhorns are curdlin. Where can I hide? Down the sewageole.

MA UBU. Sdark down there.

MEMNON. Crapnshikt, swot I do, see? One, two, three . . .

3   MEMNON, MA UBU, CONSCIENCE.

As MEMNON *dives down the sewageole,* CONSCIENCE *pops out like a maggot.*

CONSCIENCE. Fooee. My ears're booming.

MEMNON. Know what you mean. Like an empty barrel.

CONSCIENCE. Yours are booming?

MEMNON. Coursnot.

CONSCIENCE. Cracked pot, then. I'm telling you.

MEMNON. Or a potoshikt, like you.

CONSCIENCE. Excuse me, I *am* Pa Ubu's conscience.

MEMNON. Was it im threw you down the sewageole?

CONCEINCE. Oh, I deserved it. I was tormenting him.

MA UBU. Poor lil boy den.

BARMPOTS (*off, but nearer*).
His girdlenack
'Sgreatbig whack . . .

MEMNON. We better all get down, now, fast.

They all dive into the sewageole.

BARMPOTS (*off*).
Snot fooey, strooey,
'E'll give you the −

PA UBU. Stagger me sideways, get inside.

They burst in.

4   BARMPOTS, *carrying green candles.* PA UBU, *in his nightie.*

PA UBU *doesn't speak, but sits. The chair collapses. He bobs to the top, using Archimedes' principle. His nightie's all browner.*

PA UBU. The shiktpump's bust then? Is it? Is it? D'you want debrainin?

5   PA UBU, BARMPOTS, MEMNON.

MEMNON *sticks his head up.*

MEMNON. Sbust, sbroken. Slike your debraininmachine. Dunt scare *me*. Plus, by fallinere, an poppinoutagen, you've emptied arfme workforme.

PA UBU. Cornswobbit, now you've had it, bumdrop. Denackering, denoodlin, denurderin.

He drags him out and stuffs him in the bog with the BARMPOTS.

End of Act Four.

Act Five

1 PEARDROP, SWANKIPANTS THE BANKER.

SWANKIPANTS THE BANKER. I've just seen something absy extraordinary.

PEARDROP. Me too. Maybe. Snark. *You* tell *me*, an *I'll* tell *you*. What's it all mean?

SWANKIPANTS THE BANKER. I went to the station. They were openin a great big box. Gessforoo.

PEARDROP. That's easy. Pa Ubu.

SWANKIPANTS THE BANKER. And you know what was in it? A man and a stuffed monkey.

PEARDOP. How big a monkey?

SWANKIPANTS THE BANKER. What d'you mean, how big? Monkey size. You know, bout thisigh, browny fur, whity collar. Any bigger, it'd have been stretchin its soul to eaven.

PEARDROPS. Just the same with apricots. D'you know what I think, snark? They were mummies.

SWANKIPANTS THE BANKER. Egyptian mummies?

PEARDROP. Splains everythin. One looked like a crocodile. Dry skin, flat ead. The other had a big broad brow, like a professor. Beard. White hair.

SWANKIPANTS THE BANKER. What are you trying to tell me? Nehmind. The mummies, including the monkey mummy, jumped out of the case and took the tram to the Eiffel Tower.

PEARDROP. Amazing. We've just got off it.

SWANKIPANTS THE BANKER. Yah, I thought that. Amazing we never saw them.

2 PEARDROP, SWANKIPANTS THE BANKER, PA UBU, BARMPOTS.

PA UBU *opens the door, lit up by the* BARMPOTS.

PA UBU. You again! Stagger me sideways, get out of here. I told you before.

PEARDROP. This is *my* house, snark.

PA UBU. You, Bankiswanker, this is *your* fault. You're the one stuffinmymissus. Whaddyoo think she is, a pissypot? She's spectin now. Some kind of archeopteryx. Wonneven *look* like me. What do the philosophers tell us? You can't have playing around without marriage, therefore you can't have marriage without playing around. Stuff them, I say. An stuffyou, maty. Barmpots, grabim.

The BARMPOTS *start bashing* SWANKIPANTS THE BANKER.

Lessee now. Answer my questions. Are you an my missus – ?

SWANKIPANTS THE BANKER. Ow. Ooh. Ee.

PA UBU. We're gettin nowhere. He's not makin sense. How can he? He's fallen on his head. Nurdled his brainpan. At a rough estimate, his convolution of Broca's been damaged, where resides the faculty of utterance. That's right, the third convolution on the left. Consult the porter for directions. I mean, consult philosophy. 'The cause of the intellectual decline under discussion is a progressive degeneration of the cerebral cortex, resulting in an effluxion and effusion from the cells, vessels and capillaries of the spinal column.' Hopeless case. Noodlenackerin, teethtwistin, earnottin, bumsnickin, bone-grindin, marrowsuckin, thassall we can do forim. Then stakeim, denapperim, sliceim. After that, he can go and get stuffed anywhere he chooses. Don't hurt him though, I likeim.

BARMPOTS. Yeehah, Pa Ubu, yay!

PA UBU. Stagger me sideways, I'm forgettin my Conscience.

He goes into the cupboard. SWANKIPANTS THE BANKER *legs it, and the* BARMPOTS *nag after him.* PA UBU *comes out, holding his* CONSCIENCE.

3   PEARDROP, PA UBU, CONSCIENCE, CROCODILE.

PA UBU (*to* PEARDROP). Stagger me sideways, mate, are you stillere? Same with my Conscience. Can't get ridofim.

CONSCIENCE. Dear Enquirer, etc, remember the wise words of Epictetus.

PA UBU. Too late, mate. The play's too long already. We'll let epic teetus some other time.

Train whistle. The CROCODILE *chuffs across the stage.*

4   PEARDROP, PA UBU, CONSCIENCE, CROCODILE.

PEARDROP. Look, snark, what is it?

PA UBU. Goldeneagel.

CONSCIENCE. Don't be willy. It's a reptile. Entirely reptilian. Serpentine, even.

PA UBU. It's a whale then. A goldeneagelwhale.

CONSCIENCE. It's a serpent.

PA UBU. That proves it. I was just going to say so. *You're* barmy, and *it's* a serpent.

PEARDROP. Well, it's not a polyhedron, and that's for sure.

End of the Play.

SLAVE UBU

Page 84

Characters

PA UBU
MA UBU
THREE FREE MEN
SERGEANT PISSEASY
ELEUTHERIA
PEEBOCK, *her uncle*
FRIAR TUCKSHOP
JAILER
SULTAN SULEIMAN
VIZIER
SIR LOINSTEAK
FAZACKERLEY, *his butler*

Barmpots, clerks, cops, convicts, little old ladies, guards, judges, lawyers, public, techies, ushers.

Act One

1   PA UBU, MA UBU.

PA UBU *comes forward but doesn't speak.*

MA UBU. What's the matter, Pa Ubu? Forgotten it?

PA UBU. Shhhhhhhhh-ut your mouth, Ma Ubu. I'm not going to say it. It gets me into trouble.

MA UBU. Trouble? The throne of Baloney, the great big hat, the brolly . . .

PA UBU. Stuff the brolly. I can't get it open. My poofiprofsll stop it raining.

MA UBU. Lardifard. All those nobs decashed, all those taxes, maiay graicious presence in that bear-ole, sailing on that ship to Engelland, so you could say the magic word and Hoopla! Chancellorstecker, Prince of the Piggybank. And now you won't even *say* the word?

PA UBU. Stagger me sideways, Ma Ubu. What use was that word in Baloney? Billikins bashinme, Dogpile desertinme, Tsar Alexis fallininaditch an puttin the wind up poorole Cashnag, baddies banginoff guns at me, even though I asked them nicely not to, that fookybear bitin our Barmpots, me prayinupa rock, not to mention you, one's lady wife, nabbin all our loot, includin the cash we were savin for hay for poorole Cashnag.

MA UBU. Not important. Forgetitall. *I* do. If you won't be king and you won't be Chancellorstecker, what are we going to live on?

PA UBU. Ma Ubu: this pairofands.

MA UBU. You're going to jump out on strangers and stranglem?

PA UBU. No. They might hit me. Ma Ubu, I'm going to be nice
to people, *help* them. This is France, Ma Ubu, land of liberty,
which equals fraternity, which equals equality. *I'm* not equal.
But it says we're all equal. So either I kill everyone else and
be equal to myself, or I start bein a slave and –

MA UBU. You can't be a slave, Pa Ubu. You're far too fat.

PA UBU. And you're a cat. Scat! Fetch our slave-apron, slave-
brush, slaveook and slavepolish. Don't ever change. Stay
exactly as you are. Do a twirl for the lazangennelmen. (*to
audience*) Lazangennelmen, ain't she adorable? One's cookislave.
Aythangyew.

2   *Parade ground. The* THREE FREE MEN, SERGEANT
PISSEASY.

THREE FREE MEN.
   Three, three, three, we're three,
   Free, free, free, we're free,
   We three men are free,
   We free men are three,
   And this is our sergeant. Hee hee hee. Not so fast. We're free,
   remember. We do as we like. *If* we want to. We're free. If we
   don't want to get there, we don't have to. Square-bashing for
   freedom, oh no, oh no! All together now: down with the
   Sarge . . . Just a minute, we're free, we shouldn't all shout
   together. You start, then him, then me. One, two, three. Ex-
   hausting, but that's our problem. Here's the Sarge. Ignore him.

PISSEASY. Squad, shun!

They fall out and mill about.

Right. Free Man Number Three, two days in the guardhouse
for marching in STEP with number TWO. You're free,

remember, what are you? Free. Freedom drill, blind disobedience, remember WHO you are. Squa-ad, slo-ope . . . ARMS!

THREE FREE MEN. Ignore him. Talk among ourselves. Not together: you first, then him, then me. One, two, three.

PISSEASY. You still haven't GOT it. Number ONE, *you* drop your gun, Number Two, *you* surrender, Number Three, *you* look on with a smarmy free man's GRIN. All right, fa-all OUT. Left, right, right, left, left, right, right . . .

They march out, carefully not in step.

3   PA UBU, MA UBU.

MA UBU. Pa Ubu, Pa Ubu, aren't you the one, with your apron and your dinky hat? Get a nurdle on, find a free man, take your hookanbrush and start in onim.

PA UBU. There are some, running over there.

MA UBU. Pa Ubu, grab one.

PA UBU. Stagger me sideways, I'm lookin forward to this. Shoepolishin, haircuttin, tashtrimmin, matches under the fingernails . . .

MA UBU. Pa Ubu, watchit. You're not in Baloney now.

PA UBU. Queen of my cashness, shutit. *I* know what *you* don't know. When I was king of Baloney, I did everythin for nothin: glory, honour, my country right or wrong. Now I'm *charginem*: nosenackerin arfanicker, for example. Any more outo yoo, I'll stick you in a nonstick pan an *omlet* you.

MA UBU *legs it.*

Right, gerrafterem, seef they wannus.

4   PA UBU, THREE FREE MEN, PISSEASY.

PISSEASY *and the* THREE FREE MEN *are marching up and down.*
PA UBU *falls in step.*

PISSEASY. Slo-ope ARMS!

> PA UBU *obeys, with his disgusting brush.*

PA UBU. HayaHOPsa!

PISSEASY. Squa-ad, HALT. No! As you WERE. Disobey.
Qui-ick MARCH!

> *The* FREE MEN *halt.* PA UBU *steps forward.*

Oo's this ORRIBLE little man, this new recRUIT? Look at
him! Freer than any of you. His rifle, in all my years in the
service I've *never* . . . Slo-ope ARMS!

PA UBU. Yes sir, whatever you say, sir, I'm slopinit, I'm your
slave, sir, your eversoslave.

PISSEASY. I've explained this bitodrill a million TIMES, but this
is the first time anyone's actually got it RIGHT. Oo are you?
Some freedom-expert? So free you do exactly WHAT you're
told? A genius at freedom, Monsieur . . . NAME!

PA UBU. No: Monsieur Ub. Ex-king of Baloney, Lord de Lawdy,
Thane of Fourdoor . . . once. Not any more. I'm a slave these
days. Anooareyoo?

PISSEASY. Pisseasy. Sergeant Pisseasy of the Freemen's ARmy.
Except when there are ladies of the feminine GENDER
present. Then I'm Count Yourblessings. Remember that, and
use it always, even when giving me orders. You know so much
about Freedom Drill, you must be an officer. SAH!

PA UBU. Sergeant Pisseasy, I'll remember. I came ere to be a
slave. No orderin. Mind you, in my time . . . I was a sergeant
too. I was only little. *And* I was a captain. Nehmind. Byebye,
Pisseasy.

> *Exit.*

PISSEASY. Byebye your HIGHness. Squa-a-a-ad HALT!

He and the THREE FREE MEN *march off in the opposite direction.*

5   ELEUTHERIA, PEEBOCK.

PEEBOCK. Eleutheria, child, we *are* a little late.

ELEUTHERIA. Dear uncle Peebock . . .

PEEBOCK. Don't call me that, even when there's no one here.
Sir Umptiump. To stop people *staring*. Or better still, 'Nunkie
darling'.

ELEUTHERIA. Nunkie darling, it doesn't *matter* if we're late.
Since you got me this job –

PEEBOCK. Thanks to my nobby connections.

ELEUTHERIA. – as dinner lady to the Freemen's army, I've got
it sorted. I arrive late, they're starving, they've nothing to eat,
they see what a dinner lady's *for*.

PEEBOCK. That'd be fine if they ever *came* for dinner. They
don't. Why don't we stay away? Why do we come here, day
after day, to this deserted spot under this roasting, roasting
sun?

ELEUTHERIA. Uncle Peebo – Nunkie darling, *you* don't have to
come.

PEEBOCK. Oh but I do. Freemen, Eleutheria . . . they value
their liberties . . . *take* liberties. If an uncle's not strict, who
needs him? You're not free to me, you're a niece to me.
Haven't I looked after you? Everyone else goes round stark
naked, they can if they like, you wear a dress, only your feet
are nude – don't *I* see to that?

ELEUTHERIA. I wondered why you never bought me shoes.

PEEBOCK. There's only one freeman I'm afraid of. Count Yourblessings, your fiancé.

ELEUTHERIA. Give him a ball, tonight. A fancy dress ball. Oh Nunkie darling, Count Yourblessings! What a *lovely* name.

PEEBOCK. Yes. When *he's* around, I don't want you calling me –

ELEUTHERIA. Uncle Peebock. I'll remember.

6   ELEUTHERIA, PEEBOCK, PA UBU.

PA UBU. Soldiers, nothing. They're poor. I'll find someone else. A-ha! A fairy princess, with a green silk brolly and a dear old gent with a flower in his buttonhole. Nahthen, don't scaremoff. Stagger me sideways and gurdle my gob, young lady, let me take the liberty of taking the liberty of offrin my services. Nosenottin, necknackerin, debrainin . . . sorry, I meant shoecleanin.

ELEUTHERIA. I don't know *what* you mean.

PEEBOCK. Can't you see she has bare feet?

7   ELEUTHERIA, PEEBOCK, PA UBU, MA UBU.

PA UBU. Ma Ubu! Fetch the polishytin, the polishybrush, the polishyrag. Then graberfeet.

To PEEBOCK.

I'll deal with *you* . . .

ELEUTHERIA, PEEBOCK. Help!

MA UBU (*running in*). Here, Pa Ubu. All you asked for. Hang on, she's got bare feet.

PA UBU. I have to polish them. I'm a *slave*, dagnagit, and no one's going to stop me. Grabbem, debrainem.

MA UBU *props up* ELEUTHERIA. PA UBU *hurls himself on* PEEBOCK.

MA UBU. Lardifard, she's fainted now.

PEEBOCK (*falling*). I'm done for.

PA UBU (*polishing away*). Hangdock they're quiet. Can't stand noisy people. Right. Job done. Honest sweatantoil. Time to get paid.

MA UBU. Wake her up and ask her.

PA UBU. No, no, no, no. She'd give me a tip. I just want what I've earned. If I woke *her*, I'd have to wake *him*. I haven't got all day. I'll save 'em the trouble, that's what slaves are *there* for. Her purse . . . his wallet . . .

MA UBU. You're keeping it all?

PA UBU. Smine, innit? *I* polished ardforit. Not givin *you* any. *You'd* just *spend* it.

He goes through the wallet.

Fifty puntipees, fifty puntipees, a thousand . . . Monsieur Peebock, Sir Umptiump.

MA UBU. I *meant*, Master Ub, you're not leaving *them* any?

PA UBU. Ma Ubu, yoor askinforit. Punchupafroat. There's not enough. Fourteen thousand puntipees, thassall there is. And all ofem with that woman's picture on.

ELEUTHERIA *comes to and tries to get away.*

Ma Ubu, call me a carriage.

MA UBU. You're a – No. What's wrong with you? Too fat to walk now?

PA UBU. I need a carriage for this dainty creature, takerome, her dwellin, ome.

MA UBU. You've gone doolally. Being *naice* to people, *elpin* peeple. Orfit, that's what you are. What abat his nibseer, his corpsenesseer? You gointo leevimeer? People'll notice.

PA UBU. I'm busy. Earnin, slavin. Loader in the carriage.

MA UBU. What abat Peebock?

PA UBU. Stuff him in the boot. You go with er. Tend her, nourish her, nurture her. I'll grab on behind.

MA UBU. Like a footman, Pa Ubu, on a golden coach?

PA UBU. And *earned*, lass, earned, every penny of it earned. No, hang on, snot earned *yet*. Tell you wot: *I'll* go inside an nurturer, you grab on behind.

MA UBU. Pa Ubu, Pa Ubu . . .

PA UBU. Time to get going.

He gets into the carriage with ELEUTHERIA. *It rumbles off.*

End of Act One.

Act Two

1 *In the carriage.* PA UBU, ELEUTHERIA.

PA UBU. Forsooth, sweet child, you behold at your feet your devoted slave. Do me the honour of accepting my humble service, stagger me sideways yes.

ELEUTHERIA. Alack, Monsieur, that can never be. In all things I am sensible of my good uncle's instructions. I am vowed to accept no man's homage save in the presence of my uncle Peebock.

PA UBU. Your uncle Peebock. How fortunate then, sweet child, that we had the presence of mind to bring him along, stuffed in the boot of this here carriage.

He brandishes the corpse. ELEUTHERIA *faints.*

Shikastick, what's she think we were suggesting? Inere, with one's beloved Ma Ubu perched up behind to snaggle our snipes if we so much as . . . Nah, nah, nah. Lackeying, flunkeying, that's what we're after. Her unc dint say 'No', now, didee? Right, geterome, stand guard while Ma Ubu sees to er, does somethin abaht this faintin. 'No callers, no hawkers, no circulars.' Like a princess in a fairy castle. Never leave her side. Beinaslave, snot bad, snot bad at all.

2 *The hall of* PEEBOCK's *house.* PA UBU, MA UBU.

MA UBU. Someone ringing, Pa Ubu.

PA UBU. Cashooks, it's her again, our ladyboss. Dogs have bells
to stop you losinem. Bikes have bells so you can earem comin.
Bosses have bells to let you know they're stiller. 'Tingaling.
Take it easy. I won't let anyone disturb you. Tingalingaling.'
Snice, that.

MA UBU. Pa Ubu, you're her butler, her footman, her cook, her
maître-dee. She's starvineer. Ringin to see if you've ordered
up her dindins.

PA UBU. Ma Ubu, I have *not* ordered up her dindins. I'll order
up her dindins when I'm good an ready. You and I avent
etyet, avwe? She can have what's left.

MA UBU. You giviner the brush later?

PA UBU. Don't be so common. Not *ere*. That was fine when I
was king, made the kiddies laugh. But now we're grownup,
we're wiser. We know that what makes kiddies laugh can scare
the pants off grownup people. Stagger me sideways, mind,
that bell's gettin up my nose. We know she's there, she doesn't
have to keep ringing to remind us.

MA UBU. If there's nothin teat, give her somethin to drink, Pa
Ubu.

PA UBU. Right, cornswobbit. Then perhaps she'll give us a little
peace.

*He storms down to the cellar and brings up a dozen bottles, in several
trips.*

MA UBU. Nah wotsee doin? Sgon ravinmad. Twelve bottles.
Wherdee findem? I thought I'd hadem, allovem.

PA UBU. There, moon of my delight. Go an tell her nibs how
kind we are, how generous we are. Go through these empty
bottles, seef you can squeezer a glassadregs.

MA UBU, *her mind made easy, starts doing this. An enormous spider
pops out of one of the bottles.* MA UBU *screams and legs it.* PA
UBU *stuffs the spider inside his apron.*

3 ELEUTHERIA's *bedroom*. ELEUTHERIA, *corpse of*
PEEBOCK.

ELEUTHERIA. Oh woe is me! Oh help me! I don't know
  what's worse, those dreadful people who say they're my
  servants or staying up here, alone with a corpse.

She rings.

No one. Perhaps they've gone. Perhaps not even they had the
cheek to set up home in here: my home, their victim's home.
That great oik Ub. That wife unspeakable.

She rings.

No one. Poor old Peebock. Nunkie! Nunkie darling! Uncle
Peebock!

PEEBOCK *sits up like a jackinabox.*

PEEBOCK. *If* you please: Sir Umptiump.

ELEUTHERIA. Aah!

She faints.

PEEBOCK. Great. Her turn to be dead. This is ridiculous.
  Eleutheria, darling.

ELEUTHERIA. Nunkie, darling?

PEEBOCK. Stop fainting, can't you?

ELEUTHERIA. Wha-wha-wha . . .

PEEBOCK. Pardon?

ELEUTHERIA. Why aren't you dead? Sa-sa-sa-sa-sa . . .

PEEBOCK. Don't start again.

ELEUTHERIA. Sir Umptiump. I was saying Sir Umptiump.

PEEBOCK. You know how to get round your dear old uncle. I
  wasn't dead. Pretending. *Told* you I'd go everywhere with you,
  protect you, look after you. What else is an uncle for?

ELEUTHERIA. You did that for me? You rode in that boot for
me? Oh Nunkie. Right: if you're not dead, you can help me.
Pluck up your courage to the sticking point, and boot Pa Ubu
into the street. And his lady wife after him.

PEEBOCK. I can't do that. Without lifting a finger, I've paid
them six months' wages. They're loyal. Plus they learn fast. Pa
Ubu nicked my identity card, and learned it by heart. Sir
Umptiump, Sir Umptiump. You should have heard him. At
the ball tonight, to celebrate your engagement to Count
Yourblessings, I'm letting Pa Ubu do all the announcing.

ELEUTHERIA. But they don't do anything I tell them.

She rings.

PEEBOCK. Not much point in *that*, then. They're loyal. If you
want someone to boot them into the street, you want
Sergeant, Count Yourblessings. He's used to people who don't
do anything he tells them. I told him to wear his uniform.
And he'll have his Free Men too, for extra swank.

4   *The hall.* PA UBU, MA UBU.

PA UBU (*calmly*). Still ringing.

MA UBU. That's not Her Nibs. She knows we're not listening.
It's someone at the door.

PA UBU. At the door, Ma Ubu? So we're the porters. Right. Lock
the locks, bolt the bolts, padlock the padlocks and check the
potty's full. The one we keep for visitors, beside the window.

MA UBU. They've pulled the bell out of the socket. They're
knocking now. Crikey, thassaloudun.

PA UBU. Ma Ubu, take this chain, hook it to the wall, put up
the sign, Beware of the Dog. If that doesn't stopem, I'll bite,
I'll stamp on their toes . . .

5   PA UBU, MA UBU, PISSEASY.

PISSEASY *bursts the door open. Wild fight with the* UBS.

PISSEASY. Slave! I mean, captain, SAH! You're the butler here? Fine: tell them Count Yourblessings has arrived.

PA UBU. Pisseasy, Her Nibs is out. Or rather, snot her day for people. We're not letting her. No chance.

PISSEASY. H'm. Instruction manual, drill 47a. 'How to cope with MUTINY.' I'm going in to see her, but first I'm giving *you* a taste of *this*.

He takes a horsewhip from his pocket.

PA UBU. Hey, Ma Ubu, look. It's gettin betteran better. Shoepolisher, lackey, porter, whipping boy . . . Next thing I'll be in jug, and after that the galleys. We're made, girl, made.

PISSEASY. Look at the size of him. He'll take some beating.

PA UBU. Look at it, curlin and dancin, snippin my snackets . . . What is he, a snake-charmer?

MA UBU. And what are you? A whippintop?

PISSEASY. Harg, harg, I'm exhausted. Right, Pa Ubu, tell her I'm here.

PA UBU. Who are you giving orders? Slaves give orders here. Are you some kind of slave?

PISSEASY. A sergeant, a military sergeant, a *slave*? I'm a slave to LOVE. Eleutheria Umptiump, Dinner Lady To The Free, my fiancée, has enslaved my loving heart, and will soon command my BODY.

PA UBU. Stagger me sideways, I never thought of that. *I'm* slave ere. Whatever's duneer, *I* do it. *I'll* see to it.

MA UBU. Now what are you up to?

PA UBU. Don't worry, naggybag, I give you: *im.*

He legs it upstairs. The others nag after him.

6   *The ball.* ELEUTHERIA, PEEBOCK, MA UBU. PA UBU, *waltzing with* ELEUTHERIA.

ELEUTHERIA. Help! Nunkie! Help mc!

PEEBOCK. I'm doing all a Nunkie can.

MA UBU runs at PA UBU, waving her arms.

MA UBU. Pa Ubu, Pa Ubu! You're waltzing like an idiot. You've globbed all the food, you've jam on your elbows, you're not supposed to pick her *up* like that, you need that whip to spin you round or you'll fall and naggle your noggets, Pa Ubu.

PA UBU (*to* ELEUTHERIA). Ecod, how the pleasures of the dance steal up on one. I wanted to announce the guests, I know my place, but there weren't any. The door was locked. I wanted to serve at the buffet, but no one came, so I ate it all myself. Stagger me sideways, *someone* had to dance with you. And who else should it be, ecod, but your umbl sarfint . . . And even as I do, behold – all the less floor for Ma Ubu to polish tomorrow mornin.

They waltz.

7   MA UBU, PA UBU, PEEBOCK, PISSEASY, *the* THREE FREE MEN.

PISSEASY *and the* THREE FREE MEN *burst in.*

PISSEASY. Don't touch that man! He's MINE, I'll kill him in person. DON'T arrest him.

THREE FREE MEN. Don't do a word he says. Not together, separately. One, two, three.

To PA UBU.

You're nicked, you're nicked, you're nicked.

They drag him out, led by PISSEASY. ELEUTHERIA *throws herself into* PEEBOCK's *arms.*

ELEUTHERIA. Uncle Peebock!

PEEBOCK. My dear: Sir Umptiump.

MA UBU (*running after* PA UBU). Pa Ubu, I shared your bad times, let me share the good!

End of Act Two.

Act Three

1 *A prison.* PA UBU, MA UBU.

PA UBU. Cashhorns, that's better. That old uniform was getting tight round the triplets. Now look at us! Swanky new outfits. You'd think we were back in Baloney.

MA UBU. And *such* a naice hice. Just like Good King Wence's plaice. No one ringin, no one battrin down the doors.

PA UBU. And what doors, girl. None of that flabbin and glabbin in the wind. Proply made. Iron doors, barsina windows, two meals a day. *Plus* my physics set, sortin the rain for us. Every mornin it drips through the ceiling, waters our mattress. Bliss, girl, bliss.

MA UBU. But we can't go out, Pa Ubu.

PA UBU. I've had enough goinout. Trampin an trampin, up Russkiland, down Russkiland. Stagger me saideways, I'm stayineer. Slike a zoo ineer. The animals want to see us, we've got visitinours.

2 *Courtroom.* PA UBU, MA UBU, PISSEASY, PEEBOCK, ELEUTHERIA, JUDGES, LAWYERS, CLERKS, USHERS, COPS, PUBLIC.

PA UBU. My lords, lazengennelmen, thanks for comin. Guards, thanks for wearin your big moustaches, staininem with gravynscrambledeggforus. Makes a criminal feel important. Now then, hear the evidence, and silence in court.

USHER. Silence in the dock.

MA UBU. Glob it, Pa Ubu. They'll throw you out.

PA UBU. Ah no they won't. I'm guarded, innI? I've got to talk, anyway, else why are they askin? Right, your Highness. Fetch 'em in, the ones doing all the moanin.

JUDGE. Put up the accused and co-accused.

They bash them about a bit.

Name?

PA UBU. FrankUbu, ex-king of Baloney, Doctor of Pataphysics, Sir Cumference of Sphericals, Lord de Lawdy, Thane of Fourdoor.

PISSEASY. He means PA Ubu.

MA UBU. Victoria-Alice-Ethel-Hubertine-la-Pompadourubu, ex-queen of Baloney . . .

PISSEASY. She means MA Ubu.

CLERK (*writing*). Pa Ubu, Ma Ubu.

JUDGE. Prisoner at the bar, state your age.

PA UBU. Dunno. Ma Ubu had it last. She was lookin after it. She lost it. Hers as well.

MA UBU. You bastard I dint –

PA UBU. Oh shiiiii – No, I said I wouldn't. It'd magic me out of ere, and I want to be punished.

JUDGE (*to the plaintiffs*). Your names?

PEEBOCK. Sir Umptiump.

PA UBU (*raging*). Peebock! He means Peebock!

CLERK (*writing*). Peebock, and his niece, Eleutheria Peebock.

ELEUTHERIA. Oh, Nunkie.

PEEBOCK. There, now.

PISSEASY. Count Yourblessings.

MA UBU (*raging*). Pisseasy! He means Pisseasy!

ELEUTHERIA. Aah.

She faints. They take her out.

PA UBU. Nehmind, your judgeness. Not important. Get on with it: be strict, we've earned it.

PROSECUTING COUNSEL. The court sees before it a monster, befouled with crime . . .

DEFENDING COUNSEL. An honest man, pure as snow in Snowland . . .

PROSECUTING COUNSEL. You'll hear how he blackened the name, or at least the bare feet, of his innocent victim . . .

DEFENDING COUNSEL. How he knelt and begged mercy from that shameless hussy . . .

PROSECUTING COUNSEL. How he abducted her, aided and abetted by his wife-accomplice, in a carriage . . .

DEFENDING COUNSEL. That honest woman, his wife, in the boot of a carriage . . .

PA UBU. Oi. Stop flappin your gob. Who asked you to interrupt im all the time? Tell all these lies? Milordslazgennelmen, shut your faces, open your earoles, listen. One was king of Baloney, one bumped off half the world, one stuckemwith taxes, one drooled over bloodanguts. Every Sunday, debrainin, free for everyone, merry-go-rounds, ice-cream sellers. Ancient history, but it's on the record. One did in Peebockere – *and* we're callinim as a witness to confirm it – we exhausted Pisseasy with wippinus, we've still got the marks to prove it. We demand the biggest punishment you've got, but not death: you'd have to build such a gynormous big napperchopper, think of the expense. In any case, one wants to be a galleyslave, pretty greenat, guest of her Maj, hard labour, ooh I like it. And as for er, Ma Ubu –

MA UBU. Pa Ubu . . .

PA UBU. Glob it, gel. She can knit, she can sitanit. Life, that's what we're askin, we don't want to worry about the future. Oh, and a summeroliday, somewhere naice besaide the sea . . .

PISSEASY (*to* PEEBOCK). Some people just *won't* be free.

PEEBOCK. By the way, about my niece. No marriage. I'm not having her called Pisseasy. Such a stupid name.

PISSEASY. I don't want her. Fancy having an uncle who calls himself Peebock.

USHER. Ush. The court is considering its verdict.

MA UBU. Pa Ubu, they'll acquit you. I *told* you to use the magic word.

PEEBOCK (*to* PISSEASY). I'm so glad we agree.

PISSEASY. Let's hug.

JUDGE. The Court decides . . . Pa Ubu, d'you know how to row?

PA UBU. How do *I* know? I know how to drive a boat, up, down, backwards, forwards, inside, outside, round and about and how's your father . . .

JUDGE. Quite irrelevant. FrankUbu, alias Pa Ubu, the Court sentences you to life. the galleys. You will be taken from here to be ballanchained, then loaded on the first available shipment of convicts for the galleys of his Magnificence Sultan Suleiman. Ma Ubu, his accomplice, condemned to ballanchainknittin in solitary, as long as ye both shall live.

PEEBOCK, PISSEASY. Up the free!

PA UBU, MA UBU. Up slaves! Yay!

3 *The prison. Rumbling of balls and chains, off. Enter* PA UBU *and* MA UBU.

MA UBU. Fwooaar, Pa Ubu. Every day you get hunkier. That green hat, those ballanchains . . . fwooaaaaaar.

PA UBU. Wait till you see the iron collar they're making me, Milady.

PA UBU. What's it like, Pa Ubu?

PA UBU. Remember General Custard, in Baloney, the one you kept droolin over? Remember his uniform, the collar? No gold braid, you told me you dint want flash. No rubbish, neither. Stainless steel? Nah: pig-iron, gel, pig-iron, like these ballanchains.

MA UBU. You're off your nut, Pa Ubu. Ballanchains. *They're* off their nut, your ballanchains. Draggin behind you, makin such a din.

PA UBU. All the better to stamp on *you*, Ma Ubu.

MA UBU. Ooh. Ah. No, lord Ub, oh no.

4 *A holy household.* LITTLE OLD LADIES.

FIRST LITTLE OLD LADY. That's right. A big fat man's been brought here. Says he wants to be everyone's slave, let everyone boss him. Anyone who won't, he stuffs in his pocket and the boot of his carriage.

SECOND LITTLE OLD LADY. That's right. I was coming back from chapel. There was a huge crowd, outside the prison. Well, not the prison, the palace they're using, the one with the big committee. They've taken it over to keep Pa Ubu there till they've condemned enough people to send to Sultan

Suleiman. It won't take long. They've been arresting people everywhere, knocking down half the country to build new prisons.

ALL. God preserve us! God save this ancient pile!

5   LITTLE OLD LADIES, FRIAR TUCKSHOP.

FRIAR TUCKSHOP. Peace be upon you all.

FIRST LITTLE OLD LADY. Aah! I didn't hear you knocking.

FRIAR TUCKSHOP. Is it not written, 'if thou bearest tidings of mercy and joy, thou shalt not upset their bosoms, even by tapping. Thou shalt not knock'? I come to beg your usual generous charity. New poor. New prisoner poor.

SECOND LITTLE OLD LADY. Prisoner poor?

FIRST LITTLE OLD LADY. The poor are free. Free beggars. Free in the streets. Free knocking on the windows with their crutches, so that all your neighbours can see you giving charity.

FRIAR TUCKSHOP (*holding out his hand*). Spare change for the poor prisoners! Pa Ubu's said he'll barricade himself inside the prison, *and* Ma Ubu *and* his Barmpots, unless he's promised twelve good meals a day. He says he'll chuck everyone out stark naked in the depths of winter – and he's forecasting dark, cold depths – and *he'll* be snug inside, *and* Ma Ubu *and* his Barmpots, he'll be sitting there snipping his snackets while Ma Ubu knits covers for the convicts' gynormous ballanchains.

LITTLE OLD LADIES. Twelve meals. Snipping his snackets. Gynormous ballanchains. Not a penny!

FRIAR TUCKSHOP. In that case, peace be upon you all. Not to mention the other knockers who'll soon be upon you all.

Exit. Enter COPS *and* TECHIES. *The* LITTLE OLD LADIES *leg it. The* COPS *and* TECHIES *smash the windows, replace the glass with bars, remove all the furniture and replace it with straw which they water with a watering-can. The room is converted to the set of the following scene.*

6 *Prison.* PA UBU *in chains*, PISSEASY.

PA UBU. Good ole Pisseasy. Homeless, wandrin the streets, you an your raggyboys. Comin ere to me for andouts. Tough titty. Not even a coach for wedding nookies with lil Miss Peebock. She's another ofem: free, just her uncle's her prison, and *his* roof's leaky. *Me*, now, I don't go out. It's the ballanchains, see. This one, that one. They don't like rain. I've spared no expense. I've adem glued down.

PISSEASY. Ha! Don't you worry, Pa Ubu. Think you've got it easy? A bug in a rug? I'll HAVE you. I'll grab your EARS and HEAVE you.

PA UBU. You're free, incha? Free to try, incha? I'm chained to the wall. Nighty-night. I've had the streetlamps lit for you, in case the moon won't shine for you, and I know she doesn't like you, I'm a big star-gazer, me. You'll see what you'll see, all right: a big, cold, hungry nothing. One's jailer will see you out.

7 PA UBU, PISSEASY, JAILER.

JAILER. Closing time.

8 *Corridor in the seraglio.* SULTAN SULEIMAN, VIZIER, ATTENDANTS.

VIZIER. Salameesalabim. Live forever, your Magnificence. A message from Freeland. They've got that shipment at last. Two hundred slaves. Including Pa Ubu, famed in song and story, fatter than your Magnificence's fattest eunuch, and married to the no less famed in song and story Ma Ubu. Salameesalabim.

SULTAN SULEIMAN. Pa Ubu, hm. One has heard of Pa Ubu. Ex-king of Baloney. Big adventures. Eats pork, stands up to pee. A lunatic, an infidel.

VIZIER. Salameesalabim. Your Magnificence, he could be useful. Or fun, your Magnificence. Knows heaps of things. Mooniness, your Magnificence, ship-sailing. Salameesalabim.

SULTAN SULEIMAN. He'll be good in the galleys, then, wonne?

End of Act Three.

Act Four

1   *Square in front of the prison. The* THREE FREE MEN.

FIRST FREE MAN (*to* SECOND FREE MAN). Oi, what you want? You comin on parade? You doin what you're told?

SECOND FREE MAN. The Sarge told me never to come to parade. Never in the morning, never now. So every morning, here I am.

FIRST FREE MAN, THIRD FREE MAN. We are too. Here each morning. Regular as clockwork. Whatever he doesn't say.

SECOND FREE MAN. The Sarge isn't here.

THIRD FREE MAN. He doesn't have to be.

FIRST FREE MAN. It's rainin.

SECOND FREE MAN. We can get wet if we want.

FIRST FREE MEN. You're gettin soft.

SECOND FREE MAN. That's Sarge. *He's* the one not here.

THIRD FREE MAN. We can stand here if we like. On guard. In front of the prison. In these here sentry-boxes.

SECOND FREE MAN. They're free to be stood in.

THIRD FREE MAN. Sarge said they weren't to be sheltered in.

FIRST FREE MAN. You can if you like. You're free.

SECOND FREE MAN, THIRD FREE MAN. We can if we like. We're free.

2   THREE FREE MEN, SIR LOINSTEAK, FAZACKERLEY (*his butler*).

SIR LOINSTEAK. I say, what a boring little town. Haw-haw. Built of *houses*, don't you know, just like anywhere. Remarkably unremarkable, what, what? I say, I think we're here. Fazackerley.

FAZACKERLEY. Sir Loinsteak?

SIR LOINSTEAK. Take a look in the diccers, there's a good chap. Look up: palace.

FAZACKERLEY (*reading*). 'Palace: great big building with stones and fancy windows. Royal palace: same, with guards.'

SIR LOINSTEAK. This could be the place. Or could it? Fazackerley, ask this chappie if this is where the king lives. Would you?

FAZACKERLEY (*to* FIRST FREE MAN). You: chappie. Is this where the king lives?

SECOND FREE MAN (*to* FIRST FREE MAN). Tell him we don't have a king, we're free, so this isn't his palace. Tell him, you have to.

FIRST FREE MAN (*to* SECOND FREE MAN). Excuse me: *have* to? We can say what we like. So . . . sright, mate, this is his palace.

SIR LOINSTEAK. Thanks *awf'ly*. Take this: you've earned it. Fazackerley.

FAZACKERLEY. Sir Loinsteak?

SIR LOINSTEAK. Knock on the door, there's a good chap. Say we've come to see his Maj.

FAZACKERLEY *knocks*.

3 THREE FREE MEN, SIR LOINSTEAK, FAZACKERLEY, JAILER.

JAILER. No visitors.

SIR LOINSTEAK. This rude chappie looks after the kingie chappie. And he won't let us in. Can't he see we're tourists? Can't he see we're English? I say.

(*to the* FIRST FREE MAN)

One *does* rather want to see his Maj. Can't you think of something? I mean, if he's busy, if we're putting him *out* at all, we'll make it worth his while.

THIRD FREE MAN (*to* FIRST FREE MAN). There's isn't a king. There's isn't a queen. And the ones that *are* inside, they don't get out.

FIRST FREE MAN. I see what you mean.

(*to* SIR LOINSTEAK)

His Maj and Her Maj come out every morning, so that English tourists can make it worth their while.

SIR LOINSTEAK. I say, thanks *awf'ly*. Take this: you've earned it. Fazackerley, put up the tent and set out the corned beef sandwiches. They'll be here any minute, His Maj and Her Maj. Apparently they do this every morning.

4 *Prison yard.* PA UBU, MA UBU, CONVICTS, GUARDS.

CONVICTS. Up slavery! Up Ubu!

PA UBU. Ma Ubu, gimme a bitawool. To hold the ballanchains, if the chain's not strong enough.

MA UBU. Bumbrain.

PA UBU. This collar's slippin. These handcuffs are loosnin. I'll end up free, no guards, no respect, forced to pay for everythin myself.

GUARD. Lord Ubu, look: your green hat, flying over the windmills.

PA UBU. What windmills? Aah, snot Russkiland. They're not goin to hit me. Aah. An I haven't poorole Cashnag.

MA UBU. You said he was past it.

PA UBU. Cornswobbit, he shoudov etmore. My *ballanchain* doesn't eat: *he* wouldn't complain if you stole from *him*. I haven't my cashbooks andy. Nehmind, it's the Turkishes who'll be robbin me soon, Ma Ubu. Ma Ubu, tata. We need a band.

MA UBU. You've got the guards, in those hunky yellow uniforms.

PA UBU. Nehmind, we'll make do with ballanchain-clackin. Ma Ubu, tata. For me it's the ocean wave, the oars, the oars. My Jailer'll see to you.

MA UBU. Pa Ubu, tata. If you need an oliday, come home. I'll be here, in my little celly. I've knitted you some slippers. No, no, can't bearit. Partin is such sweet sorrow. I'll see you to the door.

PA UBU, MA UBU *and the* CONVICTS *jostle their way to the door, dragging their ballanchains.*

5   *Square in front of the prison.* SIR LOINSTEAK, FAZACKERLEY, *the* THREE FREE MEN, *the* JAILER.

The JAILER *starts unbarring and unbolting the door.*

SIR LOINSTEAK. I say, Fazackerley.

FAZACKERLEY. Sir Loinsteak?

SIR LOINSTEAK. Take down the tent. Sweep up the corned-beef crumbs. Make it ticketyboo. Their Maj's are coming.

FIRST FREE MEN (*drunk, waving a bottle*), Gossavctheking. Gossavim. Upismaj.

SECOND FREE MEN. Bumbrain. Snotim. SPaUbu, SMaUbu.

THIRD FREE MEN. You shut your face. He'll make it worth our while.

SECOND FREE MEN. Me shut my face? We're free. (*yelling*) Gossavetheking. Upismaj. Gossavim.

The door opens and the GUARDS *process out.*

6   PA UBU, MA UBU, SIR LOINSTEAK, FAZACKERLEY, THREE FREE MEN.

PA UBU *stands stunned in the doorway, at the top of the steps, with* MA UBU *at his side.*

PA UBU. Stagger me sideways, what's going on? Whassall this shoutin? Drunks. Not Baloney again? They'll hit me, nasty menll hitme.

MA UBU. These gents aren't nasty. No, no, noooo. Look: one of them's tryin to kiss miay raight royal hand.

SIR LOINSTEAK. Fazackerley, get down. Quick, the diccers. Look up: king, queen.

FAZACKERLEY. 'Kingqueen: someone hung about with collars, chains, cords. Carries an orb, representing the world.'

SIR LOINSTEAK. This one's a double king. I say: *two* orbs, dragging on the ground.

FAZACKERLEY. 'King of France: the same, with a big red cloak.'

SIR LOINSTEAK. This chappie has tattoos instead. Far better. God save the king.

FAZACKERLEY, THREE FREE MEN. Gossavismaj.

PA UBU. Stagger me sideways, I'm scared. Where can I hide?

MA UBU. You started it. You can't do anything right. 'I'll be a slave', you said. 'I'll polish their shoes,' you said. Now they're kissing your hands. Quaite disgustin.

PA UBU. Queen of our eart, watchout for your lugoles. Big trouble loomin, as soon as one has the time. Just at this moment, one must dismiss one's people as graciously as when one was overflowin the throne of Good King Wence. Oi, youlot, shutyergobsan lissen. I've had enough of this shriekin, so buggeroff the lotayoo. Piss off, go on, piss off.

Exeunt, bowing and scraping and Gossavaking-ing.

7   PA UBU, MA UBU, CONVICTS (*including* GRANPA), **FRIAR TUCKSHOP.**

The CONVICTS *have poured out round* PA UBU *while he addressed the crowd, and are sprawled everywhere.*

MA UBU. Well, they've gone. But oo the L R this lot?

PA UBU. Friends, colleagues, fellow-inmates, disciples, subjects.

CONVICTS. Up Ubu!

PA UBU. Not again. Start that again, cornswobbit, I'll nacker your noodles and trundle your tripes.

GRANPA. Pa Ubu, don't be horrid. We think you're wonderful. No, really. We want to honour you. No, really. So modest, really. We want to shout your name from the housetops. No, no, really.

MA UBU. Licker.

PA UBU. Dear friends, I like it. Just don't expect cashandouts.

MA UBU. They wouldn't be so willy.

PA UBU. Shutit, naggybag. This isn't Baloney. Still, since you
ask, I'll dish out some honours. Stop you nagginanfussin. Stop
you fightinanarguin who's to polish my ballanchain. Right.
Granpa, you been pickin pockets all your life, you can be
Chancellorstecker. Legless Douglas, Marchingeneral. Friar
Tuckshop, Perce the Poisoner, noodlenackerers, debrainers,
you can be Barmpots, the Barmy army, all I have to do is say
the magic word, anIsayit: SHIKT!

ALL. Up Ubu! Up Baloney! Up everyone! Shikt, oh SHI-I-I-I-I-
I-I-IKT!

End of Act Four.

Act Five

1 *Square in front of the prison.* ELEUTHERIA, PEEBOCK, PISSEASY, THREE FREE MEN, POPULACE.

PISSEASY. Comrades, this way! The day of FREEdom dawns. Pa Ubu's galleyed away. The PLACE is empty. Except for MA Ubu. She's busy with her knitting. We're free. We can do anything we like. Even OBEY. We can go anywhere we like. Even to jail. Freedom is slavery!

ALL. Pisseasy! Yay!

PISSEASY. I accept the will OF the people. On into jail! Down with freedom!

ALL. Freedom is slavery! Down with freedom! Yay!

2 ELEUTHERIA, PEEBOCK, PISSEASY, THREE FREE MEN, POPULACE, MA UBU, JAILER.

PISSEASY. Hang on. Ma Ubu. She's knitted a MASK. From the bars of her cell. The Woman in the Iron Mask. She was better without it. She was fooARGHer then.

MA UBU. Pisseasy, nay!

JAILER. We're closed. Who are you?

Noise and tumult.

Free people? Right, get stuffed.

FIRST FREE MAN. Batter down the doors.

SECOND FREE MAN. Leave them! We'll need them later, or we won't be *comfy*.

THIRD FREE MAN. Smash your way inside.

ELEUTHERIA. We demand life sentences. What's she waiting for?

MA UBU (*raging*). Lardifards! You haven't even knocked.

She reaches through the window and bashes PEEBOCK *with a water-jug, slicing him in two from snitch to shoe.*

PEEBOCK (*in stereo*). Don't fret, dear child, you're double-Nunkied now.

ALL. Home, home at last.

The door bursts open and they seethe inside. The JAILER *legs it.* MA UBU *nags it. The door shuts again, trapping* MA UBU *by her ballanchain.* ELEUTHERIA *sticks her arm through the window and snips the chain with a pair of sewing-scissors.*

3 *The forced march across* SLAVONIA. CONVICTS, GUARDS, PA UBU.

PA UBU. Fweeorg, it's cold. Bossofemall, keep draggin uss. Captain of the guard, put our ancuffs on again: it's *borin* holdin our ands behind our backs. Tighten up the neckchain, scold upere.

GUARD. Chin up, Pa Ubu. We'll soon be there.

PA UBU. If we hadn't been so skint, we'd have bought a travlin cell. At least for the ballanchain. Snot funny the way it keeps stoppin and stoppin. Wotsit stoppinfor? Do ballanchains need peebreaks?

4   PA UBU, CONVICTS, GUARDS, JAILER.

JAILER *(running in)*. Pa Ubu, we're done for.

PA UBU. Nagbucket, don't start that again. I've stopped being king.

JAILER. The bosses are revolting. The freemen are slaves. I've been thrown out. Ma Ubu's been nagnapped. To prove it, here's her ballanchain.

The ballanchain is brought in on a wheelbarrow.

They cut it offer. In any case, it'd had enough. Demanded its freedom.

PA UBU *(stuffing it in his pocket)*. Can't stand these pocket watches. Look what it's *doin* in there.

JAILER. The bosses have stuffed their wives and kids in jug. They've broken into the store-rooms, snaffled all the ballanchains. Now they're nagging along to get to the galleys before the lotayoo.

GUARDS. Me too! We want to be slaves! We've had enough. Dagnagit, we all want ballanchains.

PA UBU *(to a GUARD)*. Here, have mine. I'll want it back, mind, when I've had a rest.

The CONVICTS start loading the GUARDS with their ballanchains. Noise, off.

GUARDS, CONVICTS. The bosses! They're coming!

PA UBU. Nah, nah, gents. Grab your courage by both andles. I see you're armed and ready. *You* can face the foe. *I'm* off. Nothin to stop me. They're naughty men, by the sound ofem, and they've got great big guns.

JAILER. Cannons, Pa Ubu. Bigguns.

PA UBU. LilOobooscared. LilOoboo wantisprison, is slippers. LilOoooboooohooo.

Cannons surround the stage.

5   PA UBU, CONVICTS, GUARDS, JAILER, PISSEASY,
FREE MEN *in chains.*

PISSEASY. Pa Ubu, you're surrounded. Surrender. We WANT
your chains, your handcuffs. All you HAVE. You're free to
GO. Stark NAKED, but free.

PA UBU. Big bully. I'm off. You won't catch meee.

He legs it.

PISSEASY. LOAD the cannon. With the CANNONball. FIRE
on that lardbucket. When you're READY.

THREE FREE MEN. All together. One, one, one.

FIRST FREE MAN. Sarge, that wasn't a cannonball.

SECOND FREE MAN. It was the Third Free Man's leg.

FIRST FREE MAN. Just the left one.

SECOND FREE MAN. They've used all the cannonballs for
ballanchains.

PA UBU (*returning*). All except this one!

He bashes PISSEASY *with* MA UBU's *ballanchain.*

Take that, take that, take that.

He starts swinging a chained GUARD *round his head, massacring*
FREEMEN.

FREEMEN. Help! Help!

They leg it. Since the line of GUARDS *is chained to them, they have
to leg it too.* PA UBU *keeps yanking the chain and pulling them over
like dominoes.*

JAILER. We're saved! Look! Sultan Suleiman!

6   *The Turkish camp.* SULTAN SULEIMAN, VIZIER.

SULTAN SULEIMAN. Vizier, have the two hundred slaves arrived?

VIZIER. Salameesalabim. Your Magnificence, we ordered two hundred, but they've sent two thousand. A few in chains, the rest howling and yelling for manacles. Stands to reason. They can't wait to row in the galleys of your Magnificence. Salameesalabim.

SULTAN SULEIMAN. What about Pa Ubu?

VIZIER. Salameesalabim. Claims someone stole his ballanchain. Berserk. Says he'll pocket the lot of us. Smashing the oars and bashing up the benches to see if they're strong enough. Salameesalabim.

SULTAN SULEIMAN. Enough. Be gentle with him. Not that I'm scared of berserkery, mind. Now I see him close to, I'm staggered. Made enquiries who he was. And lo and behold, snot Pa Ubu the galleyslave. That noble brow, that peerless paunch . . . sPaUbu my longlost brother, piratenagged all those years ago and jugged in foreignlands, sept he escaped and worked his way up from the bottom, king of Baloney. Fall on your knees beforim. But don't tellim, else e'll plant his bum on *my* throne and eat *my* people. Getimonaship an getimoutovere.

VIZIER. Salameesalabim. Your wish is my command. Salameesalabim.

7   *The Bosphorus.* PA UBU, MA UBU.

MA UBU. They're going to stuff us on board like animals, Pa Ubu.

PA UBU. Fine. I'll be a watchdog. I'll watchem row.

MA UBU. Fat sort of slave *you* are, if no one'll be your master.

PA UBU. Whaddya mean? What's the biggest thing in all the world? My slobberdygobble. An oo'sits slave, its foreverslave? *I* am.

MA UBU. Right again, Pa Ubu.

8 *On board the royal galley.* PA UBU, MA UBU. *The* ENTIRE REST OF THE CAST *are galley slaves.*

PA UBU. Behold, Ma Ubu, the pastures of the sea.

GALLEYSLAVES (*rowing*).
    Row, row, row the boat, row the bally boat,
    Row-the-boat, row-the-boat, row-the-boat, row-the-boat,
    Row the bally boat.

PA UBU. Turned out nice again. We must be coming to THE END.

MA UBU. Why are they singing through their noses?

JAILER. Pa Ubu, ma Ubu, I thought you'd like it. Instead of iron masks, I gave them all kazoos.

GALLEYSLAVES.
    Row, row, row the boat, row the bally boat,
    Row-the-boat, row-the-boat, row-the-boat, row-the-boat,
    Row the bally boat.

JAILER. Will you take the wheel, Pa Ubu?

PA UBU. *Oh* no. On a boat I may be. Goin I don't know where I may be. But I'm still Ubuslave. No more orders. I want people to *obey* me.

MA UBU. We're a long way from home, Pa Ubu.

PA UBU. Fret not, dear child. We'll land one day. Somewhere

really naice. You can tell by this boat. No rubbish. Just listen
to the engines.

ALL.
Row, row, row the boat, row the bally boat,
Row-the-boat, row-the-boat, row-the-boat, row-the-boat,
Row the bally boat.

It's time to go,
To close the show.
It's time to say
There's no more play.

Row, row, row the boat, row the bally boat,
Row-the-boat, row-the-boat, row-the-boat, row-the-boat,
Row the bally boat.

Three cheers for me,
Three cheers for you,
Three hundred cheers
For Pa Ubu.

Row, row, row the boat, row the bally boat,
Row-the-boat, row-the-boat, row-the-boat, row-the-boat,
Row the bally boat.

The boat disappears in the distance.

The End.

Appendix
UP UBU

In November 1901, the Guignol des 4 z'Arts in Montmartre
(a Punch and Judy theatre) mounted a puppet production of
Ubu sur la butte ('Ubu Uphill'), a sketch using scenes and
sequences from *Ubu roi*, with added songs. The material is of
editorial interest – a characteristic example of how the Ubu
project kept growing and metamorphosing in Jarry's mind – and
it also offers actors and directors useful additions or alternatives
to passages in the main play. The characters are all from *King
Ubu*, with the addition of PUNCH (Guignol), the DIRECTOR
(M. Trombert, 'Waterspout'), two PRETTY GIRLS and two
COPS.

Prologue

PUNCH. This is great. More people here than anywhere. Arts
Theatre. It has to be the place.

He knocks. Enter DIRECTOR.

Morning, Art.

DIRECTOR. What d'you mean, Art?

PUNCH. Sorry. Isn't this your theatre?

DIRECTOR. I'm the director. Dickie-darling.

PUNCH. Punch. Glad to meet you.

DIRECTOR. Wonderful to meet you.

PUNCH. Out of this world to get – nay, welcome – my two
hundred and fifty thousand nicker. Travelling expenses, as
arranged.

DIRECTOR. Two hundred and fifty thousand? As arranged?

PUNCH. As per contract. I'm *Punch*.

DIRECTOR. I hate to wriggle, but can you prove it?
Identification?

PUNCH. Prove my identity? No problem.

He produces a stick.

DIRECTOR *(recoiling)*. What's that for?

PUNCH. Take it. Bash me on the bonce. Don't panic: solid
wood. Hear for yourself.

DIRECTOR. One, it would hurt you. Two, I didn't order one
wooden puppet, but a whole company, an entire marionette-
ménage. Your mates are all here: Niknocchio and Co.

PUNCH. Right. I'd better check who you are.

He lifts the stick.

Dickie-darling, I think you said.

DIRECTOR. If *that*'s for Dickie-darling, I'm not him.

PUNCH. Quite sure?

Wallop.

Still not him?

DIRECTOR. Ow! Yes, I'm him.

PUNCH. I'm not convinced. You *are* the Dickie-darling who guaranteed two hundred and fifty thousand nicker?

DIRECTOR. Of course not.

PUNCH. Try again.

Wallop.

DIRECTOR. Ow! Ow! Yes, I remember. Here.

He gives him three big sacks.

PUNCH. Want a receipt?

DIRECTOR. It's quite all right. Er . . . Mr Punch, I've got to talk to you.

PUNCH. Go on.

DIRECTOR. Alone. No witnesses. Get rid of of this blabberstick.

PUNCH. My friend? My brother? We're chips off the same old block. All right, if you insist. I like you.

DIRECTOR. Mr Punch, I must present you to the ladies and gentlemen.

PUNCH. Present me? To these present ladies and gentlemen? Presently. I haven't enough sticks to get it into their heads who they're dealing with.

DIRECTOR. They don't need sticks. They're big, they'll understand without. In any case, tell me, and I'll translate.

PUNCH. Dickie-darling, I can't, I just can't. Family secrets. I
have to be sure these people here can be trusted. Well, some
of them. Well, two or three.

DIRECTOR. No problem.

*He names one or two of the audience, choosing those least like the names
he gives them.*

PUNCH. You've persuaded me. You begin, I'll join in.

DIRECTOR. This is Mr Punch. He's come a long way to be
here tonight. Travelling expenses, two hundred and fifty
thousand nicker.

PUNCH. Forget it. Think nothing of it.

DIRECTOR. I need the sacks. And I'm trying to introduce you
to these ladies and gentlemen: the audience of audiences, the
crème de la crème. This is Mr Punch. What was your father's
name?

PUNCH. Stands to reason. Punch.

DIRECTOR. And his father's name?

PUNCH. You're joking. Punch.

DIRECTOR. Amazing. And *his* –

PUNCH. Ah! Now you're talking. Woodenhead.

The DIRECTOR *staggers back, bangs his head on a pillar.*

DIRECTOR. Ow! No one's called Woodenhead.

PUNCH. Of course they are. But not where *you* come from.
Want proof? Feel your bruises. Where I come from, everyone's
a woodenhead.

He sings.

In days of old,
When knights were bold,
When maids were fair
Beyond compare,
They were woodenheads, woodenheads.

Even good old Robin Hood
Was made of wood,
Was a woodenhead, a woodenhead.
Dick Turpin too
Was made of yew;
Queen Bess was oak,
And that's no joke.
They were woodenheads, woodenheads.
The grand old Duke of York
Was made of cork,
Was a woodenhead, a woodenhead.

DIRECTOR. I see what you mean. The royal race of
woodenheads. There are hundreds of them: Stan Laurel,
Rowan Atkinson . . .

PUNCH. Johan Sebastian Bark.

DIRECTOR. Virginia.

PUNCH. Virginia?

DIRECTOR. She's a creeper.

PUNCH. Ah! I twig.

DIRECTOR. You don't mind if we branch out?

PUNCH. No, that's vine.

He sings.

Jacaranda,
Give me your answer do.
Take a gander:
I'm made of wood like you.
It won't be the softest pillow,
It's made of weeping willow,
But you and I
Will grow to the sky
In a treehouse just made for two.

Enter two PRETTY GIRLS. PUNCH *and the* DIRECTOR *kiss
them exaggeratedly. Willy dance.*

Act One

In the palace of GOOD KING WENCESLAS.

WENCESLAS (*off*). Ubu! Oi! Pa Ubu!

UBU (*as he enters*). His maj. What's he want? (*aside*) Little does he know, he's for it.

WENCESLAS *comes in from the other side.*

KING. What's the matter, Pa Ubu? Too pissed to hear?

PA UBU. Yes, maj. From drinking loyal toasts.

KING. One knows how it feels. One started this morning. Ratarsed, the pair of us. Ratarsed as newts.

PA UBU. Nehmind that, maj. Whaddyoo want?

KING. Dear Pa Ubu, come over here. At this window. Next to one. Watch the Posh Parade.

PA UBU (*aside*). HaHA! (*aloud*) Right behind you, sire.

KING. Ah! The Forty-seventh Mounted Foot and Mouth. Aren't they something?

PA UBU. They're rubbish. Look at that one, there. (*shouting out the window*) Oi, monkey's armpit, have you forgotten how to shave?

KING. He looks smooth enough to one. Pa Ubu, what's up?

PA UBU. This.

He nuts him in the belly.

KING. Bastard.

PA UBU. SHIKT!

He wallops him with his stick.

KING. Take that, you pig, you dog, you louse, you chicken, you unmitigated swine.

PA UBU. Take that, pintpot, poultice, salad-bowl, squirt, stuffed shirt.

KING. One's done for! Help!

PA UBU *pokes him along the front of the stage with his stick.*

PA UBU. Babyface, pisspant, noserag, bumwipe, bib . . . Dead yet?

He finishes him off.

Ha-HEE. That's it. I'm king.

Exit. Enter QUEEN *and* BILLIKINS.

QUEEN. What's all the noise about? Oh help! His maj is dead.

BILLIKINS. Pater!

QUEEN. Husband! Sweetie. Ah. Oh, Billikins.

BILLIKINS. What's the matter, mater?

QUEEN. I'm ill, Bill. I've only two hours to live. So many blows. How could I endure? His majesty murdered, our family finished – and you, last remnant of the royal race, forced to flee, like a common catnapper.

BILLIKINS. And forced by him, what's more. That bounder Ubu. That oik. That swine. When I think how the pater larded him with honours, lorded him – for this!

QUEEN. Oh Billikins, remember how happy we were before Pa Ubu came! Ah me, what a change is here.

BILLIKINS. Chin up, mater. We'll bide our time. We'll win back our rights.

QUEEN. Ah child, for you perhaps, glad dawn. But these poor eyes won't live to see it.

BILLIKINS. What's up? She's white. She's limp. Anyone there? I say . . . ? Oh lord, her heart's not beating. She's dead. Good grief, yet another of Pa Ubu's victims.

He hides his face in his hands and sobs.

It isn't fair. Alone at fourteen years old, with such violent vengeance to bally bear.

He surrenders himself to the most violent despair. Enter GHOSTS. One goes up to him.

Good grief, what now? My ancestors, my entire family tree. I say.

GHOST. Bear with me, Billikins. In life, I was Vaslav the Versatile, first king and founder of our royal line. To you, now, I hand this holy task: our vengeance.

He gives him a big sword.

And this great big sword. Let it not rest nor sleep till that traitor dieth, till it encompasseth his death.

The GHOSTS disappear.

BILLIKINS. Right. All I need now is Ubu. That swine, that oik. If I once get my hands on him . . .

Exit, swinging the sword. Enter PA UBU.

PA UBU. Stagger me sideways, I've dunnit: king. I've got rid of the hangover, I'm ready to start raking in the cash. Then kill everyone around and buggeroff. Whoops, two dead already. Here. Hangdock there's this ole-ere to shove em in. One! Two. There'll be more to join you, any minute.

Enter MA UBU, NOBS, LAWYERS, OTHERS.

PA UBU. Bring the nob-box, the nob-hook, the nob-knife, the nob-ledger – and the nobs.

The NOBS are pushed forward, roughly.

MA UBU. Pa Ubu, please. Go easy.

PA UBU. Listen up. Royal decree. To enrich the state, I'm going to do in all the nobs and snitch their loot.

NOBS. Ooh! Aah! Help!

PA UBU. Bring me Nob Number One. And the nob-hook. All those condemned to death, I shove down this hole. Down to the Slushpile to be debrained. (*To the* NOB) What's your name, dogbum?

NOB. Viscount of Vitebsk.

PA UBU. How much is that worth?

NOB. Three million a year.

PA UBU. Guilty!

He hooks him down the chute.

MA UBU. You're so strict.

PA UBU. Next nob. What's your name?

Silence.

Answer, bogbrain.

SECOND NOB. Protector of Pinsk. Not to mention Minsk.

PA UBU. Ducky! Down you go. Next! What an ugly bastard. Who are you?

THIRD NOB. Holder of Hanover, Halle and Harrogate.

PA UBU. Three in one? No more?

THIRD NOB. No.

PA UBU. Down the tube. Next nob. Name?

FOURTH NOB. Prince Perce of Penzance.

PA UBU. Worth?

FOURTH NOB. I'm bankrupt.

PA UBU. Cheeky devil. Down the tube. Next!

FIFTH NOB. Palatine of Polock.

PA UBU. Yes . . . *and* . . .

FIFTH NOB. That'll do for me.

PA UBU. Pollocks to that, mate. Down the tube. What's biting you, Ma Ubu?

MA UBU. You're being so fierce.

PA UBU. I'm working. Making my fortune. I'll hear the list now. Clerk of the Court, MY list. MY titles. Read MY list to ME.

CLERK. Viscount of Vitebsk, Protector of Pinsk, Holder of Hanover, Halle and Harrogate. Something about Penzance . . .

PA UBU. Dopy bugger! Yes. *Well . . . ?*

CLERK. That's all.

PA UBU. What d'you mean, that's all? Ah, the hell with it. On to the lawyers. The one who'll be passing laws now, is me.

SEVERAL. Oh yeah?

PA UBU. And after the laws, the money.

BANKERS. No change, nolle prosequi, status quo.

PA UBU. Shikt. Law Number One: judges' salaries. Abolished.

JUDGES. What'll we live on? We're skint. All skint.

PA UBU. Live on the fines.

FIRST JUDGE. Impossible.

SECOND JUDGE. Outrageous.

THIRD JUDGE. Unheard-of.

FOURTH JUDGE. Beyond the pale.

JUDGES. Under these conditions, we refuse to judge.

PA UBU. All judges down the tube!

They struggle, in vain.

MA UBU. What're you doing, Pa Ubu? Who'll do the judging, now?

PA UBU. I will. Watch and see.

MA UBU. You'll bodgeit.

PA UBU. Bodgeit, splodgeit, shut your face. Who's next, now? Bankers.

BANKERS. No change!

PA UBU. No, *all* change. First off, I want half of all charges.

BANKERS. You're joking.

PA UBU. And here *are* some charges: property, ten percent, commerce and industry, ten percent, marriage and death fifty zillion each.

FIRST BANKER. Pa Ubu, it just isn't viable.

SECOND BANKER. It doesn't add up.

THIRD BANKER. Neither ult nor inst.

PA UBU. Take the piss, would you? Bring me a frying pan. I've just invented banker omelette.

MA UBU. Fine king you are, killing all the world.

PA UBU. Shikt. Down the tube! All the rest of them as well.

Jarry's note: put in topical references here ad lib.

Him, for a start, that bastard who . . . That actor who . . . That violinist with the . . . That footballer . . . That journalist . . . (*etc*) The hell with it, everyone, everyone, down the tube. Get on with it. Down the tube.

Curtain.

Act Two

Right, windmill with practicable upstairs window. L, rocks. Backdrop: sea. Enter GENERAL CUSTARD, *followed by the* BALONIAN ARMY.

ARMY (*singing*).
Ten green buttons, buttons on my shirt,
Ten green buttons, buttons on my shirt,
And if one green button should accident'lly squirt,
There'd be nine green buttons, buttons on my shirt.

Nine green buttons . . . (*etc*)

Eight green buttons . . . (*etc*)

Seven green buttons –

CUSTARD. Squad, halt! Stand at ease! AttenSHUN! Right DWESS. Standa . . . SIDE. Stand . . . EASY. Now you chaps, I'm pleased with you, weally pleased. Never forget, you're wiflemen, and there's no twuer wanker than a wifleman. Hold your heads high, march wight out to face the foe, for honah, for victowy. Weady? Ten . . . SHUN. By the wight, quick, march. Left wight, left wight, left wight, left wight . . .

He leads the army off.

SOLDIERS. Up Baloney. Up Ubu. Up Baloney. Up Ubu . . . (*etc*)

When they've gone, enter PA UBU *in helmet and breastplate.*

PA UBU. This ironmongery's ridiculous. I'll be so loaded, I won't be able to run if they're after me.

MA UBU. What's he look like? His breastplate, his iron hat. Like an armour-plated pumpkin.

PA UBU. Time to mount. Bring forth Cashnag.

MA UBU. Sorry, chum. Cashnag can't carry you. Five days, he's not been fed. He's knackered.

PA UBU. You're joking. Twelve pee a day and still can't carry me? You're pulling my leg, cornswobbit, you're pocketing the cash. Nehmind, bring Cashnag Two. Rumblestuffsticks, I refuse to walk.

BIG BAD BERNIE, *played by a Moor, brings in an enormous horse.*

Thanks, gentle Bernie.

He strokes the horse.

There, there. I'll mount. I'll fall.

The horse moves.

Help! Make it stand still. I'll fall. I'll die.

The horse takes him off.

MA UBU. What an idiot. He's on. He's off again.

Re-enter PA UBU, *on the horse.*

PA UBU. Godnagit, I thought I'd had it that time. Nehmind, I'm off. To war. I'll kill the whole world. Especially those who don't march in step. Ubu be angry, Ubu pullout oo teef, oo tongue.

MA UBU. Pa Ubu, farewell.

PA UBU. I forgot to tell you. Take over while I'm gone. I've got the cashledger with me, so keep your sticky hands to yourself, all right? I'm leaving Big Bad Bernie to look after you. Ma Ubu, farewell.

MA UBU. Pa Ubu, tata. Give that Tsar whatfor.

PA UBU. Watch me. Nose-knotting, teeth-twisting, tongue-tearing, noodlenackering.

Fanfares as he disappears.

MA UBU. Hangdock he's gone. Lardifard! Right. Get organised, snitch all the cash. Ere Bern, I need you.

BIG BAD BERNIE. How d'you mean, milady?

MA UBU. You eard is lordship. You're to take his place while he's away. His place, gerrit? My place, that is, tonight.

BIG BAD BERNIE. Oh milady.

MA UBU. Stop blushing. Willy boy. Who can tell, anyway, with a face like yours? Come and give me a hand with the treasure.

They speak the following verses very quickly as they pack:

Grab all the loot
And scoot

BIG BAD BERNIE.
One candlestick
Be quick

MA UBU.
One double sheet
How sweet

BIG BAD BERNIE.
One big bass drum
He'll come

MA UBU (*with a stirrup-pump*).
One thingumajig
It's big

BIG BAD BERNIE.
Deposit book
Here look

MA UBU (*with a dustpan and brush*).
Dustpan and brush
No rush –

Aee! What's that? He's back back. So soon. Come on!

They drop the treasure and leg it. The ARMY *crosses the stage, followed by* PA UBU *who is dragging a long bridle.*

PA UBU. Hobblit, daggit, naggit, we're passing out. It's bloody marvellous. To stop the nag knackering under us, our cashness has had to walk. Leading the bleeder.

Now the horse appears.

Just wait till we get back to Baloney. Five minutes with our physics set, our poofiprofs, we'll invent a wind-cart to waft us wherever we want. Us and our army. Hello, Nick Nackerley now. What is it? Well?

NICK NACKERLEY. Lord, all is lost. The Balonians are revolting. Big Bad Bernie's disappeared. Ma Ubu's snitched all the treasure, all the loot, and legged it.

PA UBU. So soon? Polecat! Vulture! Fruitbat! Where did that lot come from? Puddle me. Who's responsible? Billikins, betya. Where have you come from?

NICK NACKERLEY. Baloney, sire.

PA UBU. Shikt, son, if I thought this was true we'd all be on our way home right now. But see here, sonny, you've got cloud for brains. You're dreaming, sonnikins. Go to the front line. Take a look: Russkies. We'll make a sortie, sunshine. Give it all we've got: shikthooks, cashpikes, everything.

CUSTARD. Pa Ubu, look. Wusskies.

PA UBU. You're right. Russkies. Brilliant. If we'd some way out of here. But we haven't. We're on a hill; we're sitting ducks.

SOLDIERS. Russkies! Oh woe! The foe!

PA UBU. Time to get organised. For battle. We'll stay up here. No point in going down there. I'll stand in the middle. Like a living citadel. You can all protect me. Stuff your guns with bullets. Eight bullets means eight dead Russkies, eight more bastards off my back. Light armed Foot, down there. Wait till they charge, then killem. Heavy Horse, hang back, then charge. Artillery here, all round this windmill. If anything moves, shoot it. Me? Us? We'll wait inside the windmill. We'll stick our cashcannon through the window, bar the door with our poky-stick, and if anyone breaks in, they'll be really in the shikt.

OFFICERS. Sah! Sah! Sah!

PA UBU. We'll win, no problem. What time is it?

A cuckoo crows three times.

CUSTARD. Eleven a.m.

PA UBU. Dinner time. They'll not attack till twelve. General Custard, tell the men: fall out and pee, then fall back in and start the Cashnal Anthem.

CUSTARD. Sah. Weady, chaps? By the wight in thwees. Left wight, left wight.

Exit ARMY. *Impressive orchestral introduction.* PA UBU *sings. The* ARMY *comes back in time to join in the chorus.*

PA UBU.
God save our gracious me,
Long live our noble me,
Pour me some –

SOLDIERS. Beer, beer, beer, beer, beer, beer, beer, beer.

PA UBU.
Fill up your tanks and then
Unzip your pants and then
All start to –

SOLDIERS. Pee, pee, pee, pee, pee, pee, pee, pee.

PA UBU.
Soon as you've room for more
Flap gob and start to pour,
Fill up with –

SOLDIERS.
Beer, beer, beer, beer, beer, beer, beer, beer.

PA UBU. I love it. I love you all. Time for dinner.

SOLDIERS. Chaaaarge!

PA UBU. General Custard, pray order the orderlies to order in the orders we ordered.

CUSTARD. You're joking, Pa Ubu. There's nothing.

PA UBU. Catbasket, nothing? What d'you mean? Where's his noshfulness, the Maître Dee?

CUSTARD. You slushed him down the tube, wemember?

PA UBU. Don't panic. I've just remembered. It's all in hand. This administration has it all in hand. Baloney soup, calfcollops, paté de dog, turkey bum, Charlotte Russe, tartyfarts, cauliflower shikt. I'll stuff our guts meself. Scuse me.

Exit.

CUSTARD (*shouting*). What have you found, Pa Ubu?

PA UBU *comes back with the lavatory brush.*

PA UBU. Just this. Here, have a taste.

CUSTARD *and* SOLDIERS. Pooah. Fooah. I'm dead. I'm done for. Bastard Ubu.

Exeunt in convulsions. PA UBU *is alone onstage. Artillery fire, off.*

PA UBU. I'm starvinere. What on earth's to staffmagut?

A cannonball flies in and stuffs his gut. Re-enter CUSTARD.

CUSTARD. Lord Ubu, the Wusskies are attacking.

PA UBU. Sowot? Don't look at me. Snot my fault. Cashofficers, prepare for battle.

Second cannonball. PA UBU *is sent flying. The cannonball bounces several times off his belly.*

CUSTARD. Another cannon ball. I'm off.

He legs it.

PA UBU. I've had enough of this. It's raining lead and iron. Oi, Russkies, don't point that thing this way. There's no one ere.

VOICE (*off*). His Totality the Tsar!

The RUSSKIES a *make a sortie.*

PA UBU. Come on. See this stickomine? Tsar, make my day.

Enter TSAR ALEXIS OF ALL THE RUSSKIES.

TSAR ALEXIS. Stroganoff, Kalashnikoff, Ripsiskorsetsoff.

PA UBU. Over here.

> TSAR ALEXIS *snatches his stick and fights back.*

> Hey, hang on. Only joking, maj. Didn't mean it. Ow. I'm dead. That hurt!

> *He runs, with* TSAR ALEXIS *after him.* CUSTARD *crosses.*

CUSTARD. This is weally seewious.

PA UBU. Time to leg it. This way, Balonians. No, that way. Now!

POLSKIS (*racing about*). Run for it. Run for it.

> *They leg it, pursued by the* RUSSKIES. *Pause. The* BEAR *crosses the empty stage. Pause. Enter* PA UBU.

PA UBU. Have they gone? What a mob! Dogalmighty, where can I hide? Ah, that little house.

> CUSTARD *comes out of the mill.*

CUSTARD. Who goes there?

PA UBU. Ah! Oh, it's you. You hiding too? Not dead yet?

CUSTARD. Sir Ubu, how's the tewwor? How's the wunning?

PA UBU. The terror's fine. I've still got the wuns.

CUSTARD. What a wepwobate.

BEAR (*off*). WaaaRAAAGH.

CUSTARD. What was that woa-wing? Pa Ubu, go and see.

PA UBU. No fear. Lbe Balonians. I'm uptoeerwithem. Any more from them, anIstickemERE.

> *Enter* BEAR.

CUSTARD. Sir Ubu!

PA UBU. Oh look. Nice doggie. Here boy. Miaow, miaow.

CUSTARD. It's a bear, and it's weally big.

PA UBU. A bear! Weally big! It'll eat me. Dog protect me. It's coming for me. No, it's eating Custard. What a relief.

The BEAR *attacks* CUSTARD, *who defends himself.* PA UBU *hides in the mill.*

CUSTARD. Help. Help. Sir Ubu, wally round.

PA UBU sticks his head out of the windmill window.

PA UBU. Get stuffed. We're saying our prayers.
Ourfevverwichartineven. It's you it's eating: not our turn.

CUSTARD. It's got me. It's biting me.

PA UBU. For wotweerabowtoreseev.

CUSTARD, *grabbed by the* BEAR, *shrieks. The* BEAR *takes him in its jaws and exit.*

PA UBU. Thelordsmasheperd. Oh look, it's eating him, not me.
Farsunolyghostamen. I can come out. We owe our present
safety to our supreme courage and brilliance, not hesitating
for one moment to climb into this high mill so that our
prayers would start off nearer eaven. I'm knackered. Strange
drowsiness sweeps over me. But I can't sleepeer. Even with a
nightcap -

He puts one on.

I can't sleep in a windmill. Too many draughts. Geddit,
windmill, draughts . . .

Traditional tableau: night, with mice, spiders, owls, etc.

I think I'll sleep outside.

Scuttling noise, off.

It's back. The bear. Safterme. No point trying to sleep.
Hangdock I've still got my poky-stick.

Enter MA UBU. *She gets the stick.*

Ah! Ma! I thought you were an animal. Whatyoo doinere?
Where the L U been?

MA UBU. The Balonians are after me.

PA UBU. Thassalaff. The Russkies a rafterME. And when they
catch me -

MA UBU. They can keep you.

PA UBU. Ma Ubu, that does it. Debrainin, bumstrippin –

He shakes her.

MA UBU. No, Pa Ubu. Come away with me. It's not safe here. Let's emigrate. Look: the seaside. We'll take the first boat out. But where?

PA UBU. Where? Ah where? Wherowhereowhere? I gottit: Engelland!

He sings.

Land of chips and ketchup,
Sausages and tea,
That's the place to fetch up,
That's the place for me –

Ma Ubu, we'll live there happily ever after.

MA UBU. Oh yes, Pa Ubu, yes.

PA UBU. Oh look, a boat. We're saved.

Enter BILLIKINS.

BILLIKINS. Not yet!

PA UBU *and* MA UBU. Billikins! Oh no!

BILLIKINS. Ubu, you oik, you killed good king Wenceslas, my pater –

PA UBU *groans.*

You murdered her majesty my mater –

PA UBU *groans.*

You finished my family, you nackered the nobs, you jumped on justice, you brained all the bankers, but one thing you forgot; the boys in blue!

Enter COPS.

PA UBU (*terrified*). Dogelpme, where can I hide? What's tappen to Ma Ubu? Ma Ubu, you look really ugly today, is it because we've got company?

Enter BIG BAD BERNIE.

MA UBU. Bernie, my faithful Big Bad Bernie, will take me away to Engelland.

BILLIKINS. And you, cops, take away Pa Ubu. Take him to town, to a deep dark dungeon, or rather, to the slushpile, to pay for his crimes, to be debrained!

All join in the finale.

Row, row, row the boat, row the bally boat,
Row-the-boat, row-the-boat, row-the-boat, row-the-boat,
Row the bally boat.

It's time to go,
To close the show.
It's time to say
There's no more play.

Row, row, row the boat, row the bally boat,
Row-the-boat, row-the-boat, row-the-boat, row-the-boat,
Row the bally boat.

Three cheers for me,
Three cheers for you,
Three hundred cheers
For Pa Ubu.

Row, row, row the boat, row the bally boat,
Row-the-boat, row-the-boat, row-the-boat, row-the-boat,
Row the bally boat.

The boat disappears in the distance, as

The curtain falls.